THE BAKING COOKBOOK FOR TEENS

Simple Step-by-Step Recipes & Essential Techniques for Young Bakers

A Skill-Building Guide with Pictures

Amber Netting

CONTENTS

INTRODUCTION

It is never too early to start cooking. This book will help you acquire baking skills that will last a lifetime, whether you just want to bake some cookies or you're getting ready to live on your own away from home. It introduces you to basic cooking concepts while also providing 65 sweet and savory recipes that will certainly satisfy you.

If you've never set foot in the kitchen, don't worry, this cookbook's simple and straightforward guide will teach you everything you need and want to know, starting with the absolute basics such as kitchen safety, proper mixing, understanding measurement, and more. Once you have that down, get ready to impress your friends (and yourself) with delicious food.

With this tasty cookbook, you're never too young to learn about the joy of baking.

CHAPTER 1. LET'S BAKE!

KNOW BAKING BASICS

Many of you may already know these, but skim through them anyway, turning you from a beginner into a baking pro!

THE RECIPE

Read through the entire recipe before beginning

I know, I know... Maybe you're rolling your eyes at me. But if you ever dove straight into creaming butter or mixing muffin batter after only reading the list of ingredients, raise your hand. It only takes an extra minute, but it will save you time, flour, and lots of burned cookies by reading through every step.

UNDERSTAND THE LANGUAGE

Something slightly different is meant by each word, so if you're not familiar with any of the terms in a recipe, just look them up. Sliced, chopped, diced, cut, broken, beaten...

THE MEASUREMENTS

FLOURS
Everything is the same: all-purpose, whole wheat, gluten-free, peanuts, almonds, coconut, cocoa powder, and even oats. Use a fork to "scoop up" the flour from the container and shake the fork back and forth lightly over the top of the measuring cup to transfer the flour into it.

Never use the fork to 'pat' the flour down, and never shake the measuring cup either. Do NOT scoop the flour, cocoa powder, or oats with the measuring cup directly out of the container or pack them in. This results in approximately 1.5 times more than a recipe requires, which dries your baked products out and turns them crumbly. This fork technique, however, acts as a sifter and ensures that you will add the right amount of flour to your recipe!

LEAVENERS
With baking soda and baking powder, lightly fluff the leavener with a measuring spoon before scooping it out and leveling it with a knife. Some containers have a built-in flat edge, which also works!

SUGARS
Use the same technique as described for flour for white sugar, except using a spoon instead of a fork. Using a fork or spoon, lightly pack the measuring cup with brown sugar until the cup is full and level.

The brown sugar should be packed just tightly enough to hold its shape when you invert the measuring cup.

SALT AND SPICES
Like leaveners, treat them: fluff, scoop, level.

BUTTER AND MARGARINE
Most butter and margarine in the stick style are wrapped in a label with side-marked tablespoons. Count out how much you need, and use a sharp knife to cut through the stick. Because the blade is duller and you are not going to carve off as precise of an amount, you should avoid using a butter knife. Press the amount needed into a measuring spoon or cup with tub-style butter, margarine, and shortening, and level it with a knife.

LIQUIDS
A little bit trickier is milk, oil, juice, honey, syrup, and extracts. On the counter, place the measuring cup, pour in the liquid, and get down at eye level. The liquid tends to stick to the sides of the cup at the edges, while a touch of the liquid in the center sinks. For the most precise measurement, you want to make sure the center of the liquid is even with the rim of the cup. With tablespoons and teaspoons, fill them to the brim, but so that the top does not overflow or bulge.

PANTRY IN YOUR KITCHEN

To create culinary magic, baking relies on the chemistry of carefully considered and properly measured ingredients: light-as-air biscuits, chewy cookies, flaky crusts, and moist cakes. Besides good measuring spoons, fresh, good-quality ingredients are the key to baking success.

FLOURS

ALL-PURPOSE FLOUR
In most baked goods, from light biscuits and scones to chewy bread, this basic flour is a pantry staple and can be used. It is sold unbleached or bleached. It's best to store flour in a canister that's tightly sealed. It should be good in the cupboard for around eight months and refrigerated for about one year.

CAKE FLOUR
Of all the flour types, this flour has the lowest protein (gluten) level, making it great for tender cakes, biscuits, or scones. Keep it for up to eight months in the pantry.

PASTRY FLOUR

Pastry flour has a gluten level between all-purpose flour and cake flour; it is great in pie dough because it leads to a tender crust that is not extremely brittle.

BREAD FLOUR

This flour is super-high in gluten, which makes it ideal for yeasted bread where you want a lot of structure and chew. It may be found in whole or white wheat, and it may be bleached or unbleached. Up to eight months in the pantry.

WHOLE-WHEAT FLOUR

This flour still includes the outer kernel of the wheat, also referred to as the germ of the wheat. Whole-wheat flour is good in the freezer for about six months and at room temperature for just a couple of months.

GLUTEN-FREE FLOURS

A wide range of gluten-free flours, made from all sorts of grains, nuts, and starches, are available today. Most people blend a couple of different non-wheat flours when it comes to baking to mimic all-purpose wheat flour. To help imitate the chewiness normally associated with gluten, a small proportion of xanthan gum is sometimes added. For information on how to replace it with wheat flour in your favorite baking recipes, consult the specific recipe or packaging.

DRY SUGARS

GRANULATED SUGAR

This is implied whenever a recipe just calls for "sugar". This is plain white sugar, refined from beets or sugar cane. It will last for years and years when stored properly in a tightly covered canister.

SUPERFINE SUGAR

It dissolves almost instantaneously and is useful for cool liquids and meringues because it is more finely granulated than table sugar. Store it just like granulated sugar.

CONFECTIONERS' SUGAR

This is granulated sugar that has been grounded into a powder with cornstarch, also called 10X or powdered sugar. In cake and cookie icings, confectioners' sugar is commonly used and is often dusted on desserts. The best thing to do is store it in the original box.

BROWN SUGAR, LIGHT OR DARK

White sugar flavored with molasses is this soft-textured, heart-tasting sugar. Generally, light and dark are interchangeable, and which one you choose depends on your fondness for the rich molasses flavor. Keep it in the original packaging or an airtight container, very well wrapped.

DECORATING OR COARSE SUGAR

The granules are about four times the size of granulated sugar and come in countless colors. This is best used for decorating and providing a crunchy texture to add some sparkle. Store it like you would store granulated sugar.

TURBINADO OR DEMERARA SUGAR

Whereas brown sugar with molasses added back to it is fully refined white sugar, turbinado is a less-refined sugar with only the surface molasses removed. In color, it is light and usually has a larger crystal. Demerara is the English term for Turbinado sugar and denotes the Demerara district of Guyana, where the sugar originally came from. Just like brown sugar, keep it in the original box or an airtight container.

WET SUGARS

MOLASSES

The liquid that remains from refining sugar is this dark, viscous syrup. From one boiling of the sugar syrup is light molasses; from the second, dark; and the third, blackstrap, the strongest. Usually, unsulphured tends to have a cleaner flavor if you have a choice of sulfured or unsulphured molasses. Molasses may be stored in the pantry, but to avoid stickiness and pests, make sure you wipe the bottle well after using it.

HONEY

For baking purposes, select a light-colored honey with a more delicate flavor. Store it tightly sealed for up to one year in a cool, dry place. Microwave it for about 30 seconds if the honey crystallizes, or melt it in the jar in a pan of hot water over low-medium heat. Store it in the fridge.

MAPLE SYRUP

Make sure pure maple syrup is purchased, not pancake or table syrup. A measure of its color is the grading of maple syrup, the darker the syrup, thc stronger and more robust the flavor. Darker syrups (in the United States, dark amber or grade B grade A) are recommended for baking and cooking. Store the opened maple syrup in a fridge.

AGAVE NECTAR

Agave nectar is extracted from the juice of the same tequila-producing plant. It tastes similar to honey and in your baking recipes it can be interchanged with it. It can be stored at room temperature.

LEAVENERS

BAKING SODA

Also known as soda bicarbonate or sodium bicarbonate, baking soda is used to raise dough and batter as a chemical leavener. A chemical reaction occurs when dissolved in liquid and combined with an acid such as buttermilk, molasses, sour cream, or yogurt that generates carbon dioxide for leaven-baked products. Because this reaction happens immediately, it's important to bake your recipes shortly after the mixture has been mixed.

Baking soda also helps your food to brown, so even if there is no acid present for leavening, some recipes may call for it. Baking soda can last for quite a while when stored in a dry, cool place. You can mix it with vinegar to test if your baking soda is still active. You're good to go if it bubbles up.

BAKING POWDER

This leavener, like cornstarch, is composed of baking soda, an acid (usually tartar cream), and a moisture absorber. The majority of available baking powders are "double-acting," meaning they react first when dissolved in liquid and then when exposed to heat again. Before purchasing, check the date on the bottom of the container to make sure it has not expired; it will be effective for about six months once you open it. You can check by stirring 1 teaspoon into ⅓ cup warm water to see if your baking powder is still active. If it's still fizzing, that's OK.

ACTIVE DRY YEAST

This is yeast, which is dehydrated into small granules. By mixing it with warm water (about 110 degrees F) and sometimes a small amount of sugar for the yeast to develop on, it will be reactivated or 'bloomed' before use. You've probably found it in the grocery store packaged in small envelopes, but it's also available in jars. This type of yeast has the longest shelf life and can remain stored in the refrigerator for years.

INSTANT YEAST

Similar to active dry yeast, it is also called "quick rise," "rapid rise" or "fast rise" yeast, but with more porous granules that do not require the step of reactivation. This leavener works like active dry yeast for about half of the time. While baking in an oven, it can be used interchangeably with active dry yeast. Before buying and using any recipes, be sure to check the expiration date.

FRESH YEAST

Fresh yeast is very perishable and moist. It must be used by the date of expiry specified on the package, normally within two weeks of purchase. By keeping it in the freezer, fresh yeast can be stored longer, but it should be defrosted at room temperature before use and then used immediately. Fresh yeast is sometimes sold in 0.6-ounce portions that are individually wrapped, equivalent to a 1/4-ounce packet of instant or active dry yeast.

CHOCOLATE

UNSWEETENED CHOCOLATE

This is also called baking chocolate and does not have any added sugar, as the name implies. Store this chocolate for up to three years, securely wrapped, away from sunlight and moisture.

DARK CHOCOLATE

It is possible to label dark chocolate as bittersweet or semisweet. Bittersweet chocolate is less sweet than semi-sweet, but while baking, it can often be used interchangeably. Store this chocolate for up to three years, securely wrapped, away from sunlight and moisture.

MILK CHOCOLATE

This is dark chocolate with a minimum of 12 percent added milk solids. The milk solids make it creamier and mellower than semi-sweet and bittersweet chocolate, but they also contribute it a shorter shelf life – usually half a year if stored securely wrapped, away from sunlight and moisture.

WHITE CHOCOLATE

Since there is no chocolate liquor, this is technically not chocolate, but it contains cocoa butter together with sugar, vanilla, and lecithin. Store white chocolate securely wrapped for 4-6 months, away from sunlight and moisture.

CHOCOLATE CHIPS

These contain less cocoa butter than bars of chocolate, which is why, when baked, they can maintain their shape. It's best to use these where the chocolate-chip shape is what you want. Best stored tightly wrapped.

UNSWEETENED COCOA POWDER

Dutch-process powder is treated with an alkali that counteracts its acidity and makes it mellower, and Natural cocoa powder has a profound chocolate flavor.

Unsweetened cocoa powder is either "Dutch-process" or "natural".

For one type or the other, recipes are often written because they react with chemical leaveners differently. Dutch-process is always labeled on the box as such; it is natural if there is no mention of the type. Store for up to 2 years in a securely sealed container.

GROUND CHOCOLATE
This is a cocoa, chocolate, sugar, and vanilla blend, and is used in recipes occasionally. In the store or your cupboard, it can easily be mistaken for cocoa powder, but it gives very different results. Store it like cocoa powder.

THE OTHER ESSENTIALS

BUTTER
Unless otherwise indicated, recipes are written for unsalted butter. If you only have salted in the house, omit any salt that might appear in the recipe. Store in the fridge, following the manufacturer's recommendations.

HEAVY CREAM
Heavy cream (also called heavy whip cream) has, with at least 30 percent, one of the highest fat contents of creams available in your grocery store. You need at least 30% fat for the cream to whip properly. The ultra-pasteurized cream will not whip well unless it contains additives. Store in the fridge, as recommended by the manufacturer.

EGGS
Recipes, unless otherwise noted, are written for large eggs.

VANILLA EXTRACT
For the best taste, use a pure vanilla extract, but an artificial one can be used in a pinch. Store in the original packaging, away from dampness.

SALT
Unless otherwise specified, most baking recipes are written with a fine-grain salt. Sometimes larger granules are also desired for added texture and crunch. Store tightly sealed, away from dampness, and it will last forever.

BAKER'S TECHNIQUES AND SKILLS

Many bakers who are just starting have questions about commonly used phrases in recipes. Even if you're familiar with this vocabulary for baking, knowing why these techniques are important can be helpful. For bakers of all levels to use as a reference, what follows is a guide to common baking terms and phrases.

ADDING EGGS, ONE AT A TIME
They should be added 1 at a time, then each thoroughly beaten before adding the next, to let creamed butter/sugar mixture retain its trapped air most effectively. Scrape the sides of the bowl to incorporate all of the butter/sugar mixture.

BAKING IN BATCHES
After you remove a cookie sheet from the oven and transfer the baked cookies to a cooling rack, before putting more cookie dough on it, make sure the pan has cooled to room temperature. Putting dough on hot pans causes spreading or losing its shape before it enters the oven, increasing the risk of burning edges and flat cookies.

CREAMING
It's the process that starts a lot of cookie recipes; when you beat sugar and fat together to form and capture air bubbles. Bubbles form when the edges of sugar crystals are cut into fat molecules to make an air pocket. The mixture is thick and slightly lumpy when you start beating sugar and fat together for the first time. As continue to beat, the mixture becomes

creamier in texture, lighter in color, and uniform as the air beats in.

FOLDING

With a whisk, sifted dry ingredients are folded into beaten egg whites. Draw the whisk in a circular motion down through the bowl and back up. Air-beaten ingredients, such as beaten egg whites or whipped cream, are combined in a way that retains as much of the air bubbles as possible with the rest of the ingredients of a recipe. For this, it's good to use a whisk, because, in just a few strokes, the many wires of the whisk effectively combine the two mixtures. In the finished product, this results in a light texture.

GREASING A PAN

You can save a lot of heartbreak (and cookie-break) by properly preparing your baking pan before filling it). For quick, effective coverage, we recommend using a non-stick pan spray, but a thin coat of vegetable shortening also does the trick.

GREASING A PAN WITH COOKING SPRAY

Hold can upright and pan perpendicular to it when using pan spray; that way you'll get more even coverage, and less sputtering from the can.

GREASING A PAN WITH SHORTENING

Spread evenly with a piece of waxed paper or a pastry brush when using shortening.

LEVELING (SMOOTHING) THE CRUST

Having crust, batter, or filling level before the pan goes into the oven is very important when baking layered or bar cookies. Uneven batter will bake unevenly; it is possible to burn one section, while the other is underdone.

ROLLING OUT

This process involves flattening chilled dough to an even thickness with a rolling pin, to be cut before baking into shapes.

An important first step is to dust the work surface and your rolling pin with flour. A big, thin spatula and a ruler or tape measure are a good idea to have on hand before you start. The spatula helps you frequently pick up the dough to keep it from sticking, and the measuring instruments help you keep track of the dimensions and thickness of the dough as you work.

From the center of the dough, roll to the edges, tending to toughen the gluten of the dough. It's helpful to place a plastic wrap layer between dough and the rolling pin if the dough is soft or sticky and to place the dough on parchment before rolling.

ROLLING INTO A BALL

Some cookies, such as snickerdoodles, are shaped into balls before being rolled in sugar to coat them evenly. With a cookie scoop, which portions approximately spherical amounts to begin with, this method is made simpler.

SIFTING FLOUR

Sifted flour, sometimes in conjunction with other dry ingredients, is passed through a strainer or screen to aerate it. In recipes where a light, spongy texture is desired, sifted flour is usually folded in with moist ingredients.

STRAINING UNSWEETENED COCOA

After measuring and before adding it to your mixture, push the cocoa powder through a strainer. Cocoa butter is found in unsweetened cocoa, which can cause it to clump. It's best to strain it to ensure it combines evenly with the rest of the dry ingredients in your recipe.

STIR

Whisk the dry ingredients together, next add them to the wet ones, stirring until mixed evenly.

ICING, GLAZE, AND FROSTING TECHNIQUES

Every kind of cake has its ideal match. Is there a difference between them? And are there various forms of each one?

BUTTERCREAM FROSTING
There's a reason for the popularity of Buttercream Frosting. It's simple to make at its most basic: just "cream" the butter (meaning beat it for several minutes), then add sugar and a hint of vanilla and salt! This frosting is easy to spread, light, fluffy, and neutral tasting, and complements all kinds of cake and cupcake flavors.

WHIPPED CREAM FROSTING
Similar to plain whipped cream, whipped cream frosting is made with confectioners' sugar and vanilla added for flavor and sweetness, and a little tartar cream (about 1/2 teaspoon for each pint of cream) for stability. This frosting is a nice choice for stacked berry cakes because it's neutral in flavor and super airy and light.

ICING
Another popular cake and cookie topping that is thinner than frosting, but thicker than a glaze, is icing (including the popular chocolate icing called ganache). Although glazes set quickly and stiffen as they dry, because of their lower sugar content, glazes also set but do not harden. Instead of being spread like frosting, icings and glazes are poured or spooned over cakes and other confections (like cinnamon buns).

ROYAL ICING
Easy Royal Icing, another favorite among professional bakers, hardens quickly and brightly and is often used to decorate sugar cookies and fancy tiered cakes. It's best to use pasteurized eggs for this icing because it uses raw egg whites.

GLAZE
A simple blend of sugar and liquid, such as milk, lemon juice, or water, a glaze can be made in a variety of consistencies that dry to varying degrees of stiffness but do not harden. Drizzle your favorite glazes over tea cakes, buns, cookies, doughnuts. From pomegranate to matcha, white chocolate, and beyond, glazes can also be flavored in all kinds of ways!

PIPING TECHNIQUES

Whether you're new to cake decoration or just want to brush up on your piping skills, these 9 beginner pipe techniques are all you need to get started. From classic cupcake swirls to piped buttercream flowers and borders, these simple cake pipe techniques are sure to attract you to icing!

HOW TO FILL A PIPING BAG WITH FROSTING?
There are two ways to do this. One way is to fold the bag over the top of your hand, and the other way is to fold it over a glass. Folding it over a glass is very helpful if you want to fill it with something pourable or hot, like hot fudge.

In both methods, there are a few useful tips to make it easier for you to fill a piping bag, whether it's frosting or glaze.

1. To create a pocket for the air to escape, first cut off the very tip (less than half an inch) of the bag. That way, when you press the frost into your bag, there's a place for the air to escape.
2. Fold the bag over your hand (or glass) at least halfway down, ensuring that the top edge is clear and folded all the way down so that you can keep it clean.
3. Use the side of your hand or the side of your glass to scrape the frost off the spatula.
4. A piping bag is folded over one hand while a spatula is used on the other side to fill the bag.
5. Use your spatula once the frosting is in the piping bag to further press the frosting down into the bag.

6. Pick it up and give it a solid shake to help further settle the frosting in the bag once the bag is filled halfway.

7. Use the side of your hand or a rolling pin to press all the frosting down into the bag once your piping bag is filled. To keep my bags closed, I like using rubber icing bag ties.

WHAT SIZE DO PIPING BAG DO I NEED?

A 12-inch bag is the smallest size I recommend using. To get that nice and fine drizzle of chocolate over cookies or a slice of cake, they work great. They're also great for writing letters on cakes, piping buttercream with finer details, and decorating royal icing cookies.

An 18-inch bag is the largest size that I use and it's the most common size I use. Because they contain a lot of frosting, they are great for frosting cupcakes and cakes, so you may only need one bag. 16-inch piping bags will also work if you can't find 18-inch bags.

HOW TO USE A PIPING BAG WITH A COUPLER:

A coupler is two pieces of plastic used together with a piping bag (similar to a nut and bolt) so that the piping tips can be changed seamlessly. The piping tip is also secured to the bag.

The trick is to only cut the bag enough so that the coupler fits through the opening, but high enough that your piping tip doesn't interfere with it.

Place the larger piece in the piping bag, then fit the piping tip over the top. Then take the smaller piece and slide it over the tip, screwing it onto the piece of plastic. Inside the coupler, you can see the bag is secured.

When you've finished, cut the piping bag 1 inch above the top of the coupling and flip it inside out to remove the coupler from your bag. Running it under warm water would help to loosen it up.

HOW TO USE A PIPING BAG WITHOUT A COUPLER:

You can use a large coupler for big tips, including 1M, but I find it's not necessary. They do not fit on the coupler when I use my large piping tips, so I drop them straight into the piping bag. Then I cut off the tip of the bag high enough so that it does not interfere with the actual piping tip. If you cut the piping bag too high, you might find that the frosting tip will pop out with the pressure of squeezing the bag, so don't cut it higher than you need.

HOW DO YOU CHANGE PIPING TIPS?

It's super easy if you're using a piping bag with a coupler! Just unscrew the outer piece of plastic, pop the tip off, replace it with a new tip, and then screw the top back on. When you want to use the same color with various tips, this is the fastest way to do it.

HOW TO PIPE A 1M SWIRL

Using a 1M decorating tip, master the classic cupcake swirl. Perfect for topping pies, cupcakes, cakes, and more, buttercream or stabilized whipped cream frosting is easy to do with this piping technique. For a different look and texture, you can also switch decorating supplies and use tip 2A or tip 2D.

HOW TO PIPE A STAR

Perhaps one of the most versatile and easiest piping techniques for beginners is the star. What's great about a star is that this tip does all the work for you... just squeeze and pull away. You can use this piping technique to fill in a large character cake with frosting with a large variety of star tips available or as a border.

HOW TO PIPE A ROSETTE

Rosettes create beautiful floral accents and are a fast and simple way to decorate your desserts. Although these are traditionally made with star tips, you can also pipe rosettes for different petal effects with drop flower tips. Use standard tips to add small rosettes to a flower-covered cake, or to pipe large rosettes, and use larger decorative tips such as 1M or 2D to bring your cupcake to another level.

HOW DO YOU FROST CUPCAKES WITH A PIPING BAG?

It can depend on how you intend to frost your cupcake, but generally speaking, you want to hold the bag over the top of your cupcake at a 90-degree angle and work from the outside edge.

HOW TO MELT CHOCOLATE

MELTING ON THE STOVETOP

The preferred method is melting chocolate on the stovetop. A double boiler gives you the best heat control. The chocolate is gently melted by the steam from the simmering water so that it does not burn.

By bringing a medium pot a little less than halfway filled with water to a simmer, develop a double boiler. Place a big enough heatproof bowl to sit on top of the pot and place the chopped chocolate bar or chocolate chips into the bowl. Keep the pot warm and stir the chocolate with a rubber spatula until the chocolate is silky smooth.

MELTING IN THE MICROWAVE

The quicker of the two methods is melting in the microwave, but it is still important to watch it carefully. Put the chocolate in a heatproof bowl and microwave for 30 seconds at a time, stirring after each time. When the chocolate looks almost melted with just a few lumps, just stir until it is completely smooth. Don't microwave it again.

While microwaving, adding a tablespoon of coconut oil or vegetable oil helps the chocolate melt more smoothly and makes it the ideal dip consistency!

EQUIPMENT YOU WILL NEED

KITCHEN SCALE
A kitchen scale in a baker's kitchen is a relatively small investment, but it is really valuable. Measurement by weight is a much more accurate way to measure, and because baking is an exact science, it is often important.

MEASURING CUPS & SPOONS
In addition to measuring spoons, you'll want to have two sorts of measuring cups: liquid measuring cups and dry measuring cups. If you're going to measure by volume, you will make the most of it by using the right cups.

MIXER (HAND OR STAND)
A hand mixer is a relatively inexpensive investment and will get you through most situations where a mixer is needed. A stand mixer is very nice to have, especially if you're an avid baker, but it's not essential.

There are a few baking applications where a mixer is necessary. For example, you'll never be able to make butter properly without a blender. You can choose either a hand or stand mixer - you don't need both of them.

WHISK

A whisk is needed to mix eggs, whip the air in egg whites or heavy cream, make emulsions like Ganache or Hollandaise, combine dry ingredients thoroughly, and aerate flour instead of sifting it.

RUBBER SPATULAS

It is nice to have rubber spatulas with rounded heads that are almost spoon-like. But as long as your kitchen has at least one spatula of any kind, you're good to go!

HALF SHEET PANS OR COOKING SHEETS

I'm not a fan of the flimsy cookie sheets you can purchase from target stores or grocery stores, and I don't have one. That said, if you already have a couple of baking sheets that you love and use, they will do just fine! You just need a couple of baking sheets, and if you need to purchase new ones, I highly suggest getting the sheet pans.

Half sheet pans conduct heat evenly, and without slipping out of your hand, the lip around the pan makes it easy to grab and pull from the oven. These pans also work well in setting up a cake pan or loaf pan that you put in the oven. This ensures that any possible overflow is captured by the sheet pan and also makes it easier to draw the baked good from the oven

MIXING BOWLS

You're often going to need several mixing bowls at the same time. I suggest investing in a stainless set that comes in different sizes. You don't need anything fancy, just a good variety of good quality.

SIEVE OR SIFTER

In every section, there will most likely be recipes that will either call for sifting ingredients or for straining them through a sieve. I highly suggest investing in a sieve over a sifter if you do not have either of these tools, because it can be used for both wet and dry ingredients.

OVEN THERMOMETER

Each oven varies and ovens are very often not properly calibrated. The best way to test if your oven is heating up to the set temperature, or running too hot or cold, is to use an oven thermometer.

Baking temperatures are capable of making or breaking a recipe. I know, for example, that I have to set my oven temperature about 10 degrees F higher than a recipe because it's not getting hot enough. For successful baking, an oven thermometer is important.

OTHER EQUIPMENT THAT IS NICE TO HAVE

The following equipment is not essential for every course in baking school but will be helpful:

1. 9 x 13″ Baking Pan (for brownies, sheet cakes, coffee cakes, cookie bars, breakfast casseroles, etc.)
2. Ramekins (for measuring out ingredients, individual souffles, parfaits, mousses, creme brulee, etc.)
3. Pastry Blender (for cutting in fat for biscuits, scones, pie & pastry crusts)
4. Bench Scraper (for transferring pastries & bread to baking sheet/dish, scraping bowl clean, scraping counter clean, smoothing out cake icing, etc.))
5. Cooling Rack (for cooling cakes, muffins, cookies, pastries, etc.)

KITCHEN SAFETY

Home baking is great fun, but in the kitchen, it is also important to be safe. There are many potential threats to be aware of, so here are some helpful safety tips:

HEAT
You usually need to use an oven and sometimes a stovetop for baking. If they are in use, be aware of the stovetop and the oven door. To remove hot pots from the stovetop or baking pans from the oven, use oven gloves or cloths. When opening the oven door, watch out for steam or hot air. Place hot food on a heat-resistant, stable surface.

WASH YOUR HANDS AFTER HANDLING MEAT PRODUCTS
It's important to prevent cross-contamination when handling meat products of any kind. Washing your hands with soap is one easy way to do this. Be sure to scrub them well and for a minimum of 20 seconds!

CLOTHING
When you are baking, it's a good idea to wear an apron and a closed shoe. This will keep you and your clothes clean, and your feet safe from spills or falling objects. Keeping your hair tied back away from your face is also a good idea to prevent it

from getting in the way and falling into the food you are making.

KEEP COUNTERTOPS CLEAN

Many recipes for holiday cookie dough require you to roll your dough on the counter. I recommend that a sanitizing spray or rinse for cleaning counters be used before and after doing so. To keep your baking workspace safe and clean, you can clean it with a mix of one teaspoon of bleach into 1 quart of water, or any other solution.

SHARP IMPLEMENTS AND EQUIPMENT

Baking often requires the use of beaters, mixers, knives, and other hazardous devices and equipment. Be careful when using sharp knives. Never put your hand into a mixer or any other turned on or moving equipment. Before touching electrical switches, make sure your hands are dry. If you cut yourself, clean the wound and apply a plaster before you continue baking.

DON'T LET PERISHABLE INGREDIENTS SIT ON THE COUNTER FOR TOO LONG

Anything that comes from the fridge needs to stay in the fridge as long as possible. So, when baking, resist the urge to keep eggs, milk, and other perishable items on the counter. Instead, keep them cool in the fridge.

STORAGE

Store the ingredients and equipment for baking in such a way that they are easy to reach and will not fall on you or anyone else. Keep ingredients covered, preferably in a sealed container to keep them fresh and free from contamination.

WASH YOUR UTENSILS AND BAKING SHEETS WELL

This, again, is all about avoiding cross-contamination. So, after every single use, wash your utensils, baking sheets, and bowls well!

SPILLS

Clean up immediately if you spill ingredients on the floor to avoid slipping.

MISTAKES AND TIPS TO BAKE LIKE A PRO

YOU USE BAKING POWDER INSTEAD OF BAKING SODA (OR VICE VERSA).

It is very tricky to substitute one for the other. This is partly because, to act as a leavening agent, baking soda needs an acid to react to (like lemon juice or vinegar). Meanwhile, in addition to tartar cream, which is already an acid, the baking powder contains baking soda. They're not interchangeable, so long story short, you should always have both in your pantry.

YOU DON'T USE ROOM TEMPERATURE BUTTER WHEN YOUR RECIPE CALLS FOR IT.

Baking is science, so your ingredients' temperature is important. If you have forgotten to take the butter out of the fridge in advance, just warm a glass bowl in the microwave and cover the butter with it for a few minutes. This will make it softer and accelerate the process.

YOU START WORKING ON CAKE BATTER WITHOUT HAVING PREPARED YOUR PAN BEFORE.

Look, we have all been there. In the recipe, we read the line about preparing our pan, but we would prefer to get straight into the making, so we skip this step and prepare our pan last-minute when the batter is ready. That's no good.

Once your cake batter is ready you need to put it in the oven immediately to ensure that the leavening agents can do their work (especially if you are using baking soda). This is why, before you begin anything else, you should prepare your tin.

WHEN YOU CREAM BUTTER AND SUGAR, YOU STOP HALFWAY THROUGH.

First, make sure your butter is just at room temperature when you're creaming your sugar and butter together. Second, once the butter and sugar have just come together homogeneously, don't stop beating. You should keep beating at medium speed (3-4 on a stand mixer) until it's fluffy and lighter in color. Roll a bit of the mass in your fingers to see if it is ready. You're good to go if there's barely any sugar granules left in it.

YOU THINK YOU DON'T NEED TO ADD A PINCH OF SALT TO YOUR BATTER.

In desserts, you may think salt is not necessary, but it is. Salt helps to improve the flavor and sharpen your cakes' sweetness, so always make sure to add a little to the mix.

YOU DON'T SIFT DRY INGREDIENTS WHEN THE RECIPE TELLS YOU TO.

Sifting can be an unnecessary extra step for some cakes, but make sure you do so if the recipe says so. It will help to integrate the dry ingredients into the rest of the mixture uniformly and avoid any large clumps.

YOU DON'T PREHEAT YOUR OVEN.

It is crucial to bake your cake/cookies/pie at the right temperature. When you start cooking, if the oven is too cold, it might prevent your cake from rising or browning properly. So, before starting anything else, preheat your oven.

OPEN YOUR OVEN DOOR WHILE BAKING.

The temperature of the oven goes down every time you open the oven door. This will stop your cake from rising as well as it could and slow down the process of baking. So, be patient and, if necessary, look through the door, but keep the door shut until that timer goes off.

YOU DON'T WAIT FOR YOUR CAKE TO COOL DOWN BEFORE DECORATING IT.

Patience is also fundamental here. If the buttercream is put on a warm cake, the frosting will melt. So, cool your cake completely before you begin to decorate it.

CHOCOLATE CHIP COOKIES

SERVINGS: 20 | PREP TIME: 10 min. | COOK TIME: 20 min.

CARBS: 29 g | FAT: 11 g | PROTEIN: 3 g | CALORIES: 226

INGREDIENTS

- 1 cup caster sugar
- 2 cups plain flour, sifted
- 1 cup melted butter
- 1 tsp vanilla extract
- 1 tsp baking powder
- 1 pinch of salt
- 1 egg
- 1 cup chocolate chips

DIRECTIONS

1. Mix the sugar and butter in a bowl.
2. Sift the baking powder, flour, vanilla, and salt, then add to the butter mixture. Add the chocolate chips. Mix with your hands to get a dough texture. Add the egg and knead.
3. Spread some butter onto a baking tray. Take a bit of the dough, roll into a ball and flatten a little. Don't forget to leave enough free space between them.
4. Bake for 10-20 minutes at 320°F. The time depends on the size of the cookies – the bigger cookie, the longer it will take to bake them. If the edges are a bit golden, the cookies are ready.

PEANUT BUTTER CHOCOLATE CHIP BARS

SERVINGS: 9 | PREP TIME: 10 min. | COOK TIME: 50 min.

CARBS: 45 g | FAT: 21 g | PROTEIN: 5 g | CALORIES: 379

INGREDIENTS

- ½ cup unsalted butter, melted
- ⅓ cup peanut butter
- 1 large egg
- 1 cup all-purpose flour
- 1 cup light brown sugar, packed
- 1 Tbsp vanilla extract
- 1 cup chocolate chips + 2 Tbsp, for sprinkling

DIRECTIONS

1. Preheat the oven to 350°F. Using foil, line an 8x8-inch baking pan, lightly oil it with cooking spray.
2. Melt the butter for 1 minute in a microwave-safe bowl on high power. Wait 1-2 minutes before adding the egg or you will scramble it. Whisk in the egg, peanut butter, sugar, and vanilla and mix until smooth. Add the flour and mix until just combined. Stir in the chocolate chips.
3. Turn the prepared batter out into the prepared pan and lightly smooth the top with a spatula. Sprinkle with 2 Tbsp chocolate chips.
4. Bake for 20-25 minutes until done. A toothpick inserted in the center should be clean and come without any batter on it.
5. Let the bars cool in the pan for at least 30 minutes before slicing and serving.

CHRISTMAS CRINKLE COOKIES

SERVINGS: 30 | PREP TIME: 20 min. | COOK TIME: 1 h. 10 min.

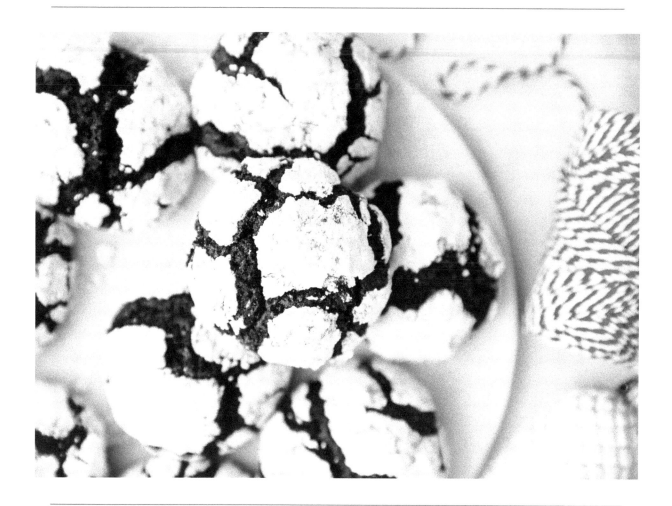

CARBS: 13 g | FAT: 3 g | PROTEIN: 2 g | CALORIES: 88

INGREDIENTS

- ½ cup cocoa powder, sieved
- 1 cup caster sugar
- 3 Tbsp vegetable oil
- 2 large eggs
- ½ cup plain flour
- 1 tsp baking powder
- 2 oranges, zested
- 2 tsp mixed spice
- 1 tsp cinnamon
- ½ cup icing sugar
- 1 pinch of salt

DIRECTIONS

1. Mix the cocoa, oil, and caster sugar in a bowl. Whisk in the eggs – one at a time – until fully combined.
2. Mix the baking powder, spice mix, flour, orange zest, cinnamon, and salt in another bowl, then add it to the prepared cocoa mixture and mix until you get a soft dough. If it's too soft, put it in the fridge for 1 hour to chill.
3. Preheat the oven to 380°F and add the icing sugar to a shallow dish. Roll heaped tsps of dough into balls, then roll them in the icing sugar to make a coating. Transfer the balls onto a large baking tray lined with baking parchment, leaving free space between the cookies.
4. Bake for 10 minutes in the oven on the middle rack, then transfer the cookies to a wire rack to cool until they are firm.

LEMON BARS

CARBS: 36 g | FAT: 9 g | PROTEIN: 3 g | CALORIES: 239

INGREDIENTS

For the crust:
- 2 cups + 2 tbsp all-purpose flour
- 1 cup powdered sugar
- ½ tsp salt
- 1 tsp vanilla
- 1 cup unsalted butter, melted

For the filling:
- 2½ cups granulated sugar*
- ½ cup all-purpose flour
- 7 large eggs
- 1 cup fresh lemon juice
- Pinch salt

DIRECTIONS

1. Preheat the oven to 350°F, cover the bottom and sides of a 9x13-inch baking pan with parchment paper.
2. To make the crust, mix the flour, powdered sugar, and salt in a bowl. Add the melted butter and vanilla, mix to combine.
3. Crumble and arrange the prepared crust mixture over the bottom of the pan and press it evenly into the bottom.
4. Bake for 14-19 minutes until the edges start getting a little browned. Take it out of the oven and set aside.
5. Mix the sugar and flour for the filling in a bowl. Add the eggs, lemon juice, and salt and whisk just to combine.
6. Pour the filling on top of the crust and bake for 18-22 minutes. Take out of the oven and cool for 30 minutes. Put in the fridge until cold and firm.
7. Once done, remove the bars from the pan, dust with powdered sugar, and cut into squares before serving.

CHOCOLATE BROWNIES

SERVINGS: 9 | PREP TIME: 5 min. | COOK TIME: 30 min.

CARBS: 23 g | FAT: 11 g | PROTEIN: 4 g | CALORIES: 212

INGREDIENTS

- ⅔ cup all-purpose flour
- ½ cup unsweetened cocoa powder
- ¼ tsp salt
- ½ cup unsalted butter (1 stick)
- 2 Tbsp coconut oil, melted with butter
- 1¼ cups sugar
- 2 large eggs
- 1 Tbsp vanilla extract

DIRECTIONS

1. Preheat the oven to 350°F. Grease an 8x8-inch square baking pan.
2. Mix the cocoa, salt, and flour in a bowl and set aside.
3. Melt butter in the microwave in a large microwavable bowl.
4. While the butter is hot, mix it with oil and sugar, whisk until mixed.
5. Add the eggs and vanilla and mix to combine. Add the flour and whisk again to combine.
6. Pour the prepared batter into the greased pan and spread it evenly.
7. Bake for 28-30 minutes until a toothpick comes out clean or with a few crumbs.

SALTED CARAMEL CHOCOLATE CHIP COOKIE

SERVINGS: 30 | PREP TIME: 16 min. | COOK TIME: 30 min.

CARBS: 39 g | FAT: 13 g | PROTEIN: 3 g | CALORIES: 285

INGREDIENTS

- *1 cup unsalted butter, softened*
- *1 cup packed light brown sugar*
- *½ cup granulated sugar*
- *2 large eggs*
- *1 tsp vanilla extract*
- *1 tsp kosher salt*
- *1 tsp baking soda*
- *2½ cups all-purpose flour*
- *2 cups chocolate chips*
- *14 ounces sweetened condensed milk*
- *10 ounces soft caramels, unwrapped*
- *1 tsp flaked sea salt*

DIRECTIONS

1. Preheat the oven to 350°F. Line a 9x13-inch baking dish with foil and lightly coat it with cooking spray.
2. Beat the butter and sugars with an electric mixer for 2 minutes until light and fluffy. Add the vanilla, eggs, salt, and baking soda. Mix well, then scrape all sides of the bowl with a spatula.
3. Set to low speed and gradually add the flour. Beat until well combined, then stir in the chocolate chips.
4. Press half the dough into the bottom of the foil-lined baking dish.
5. Add the sweetened condensed milk and caramels to a saucepan. Cook and stir over a medium-low heat until the caramels melt to get a smooth caramel mixture. Pour it over the cookie dough base.
6. Drop the second half of the dough over caramel in teaspoon-sized clumps. Put in the oven and bake for 25-30 minutes.
7. Sprinkle with salt and cool completely. Lift the chilled bars out of the pan using the edges of the foil and cut.

PEANUT BUTTER COOKIES

SERVINGS: 16 | PREP TIME: 15 min. | COOK TIME: 12 min.

CARBS: 12 g | FAT: 7 g | PROTEIN: 4 g | CALORIES: 126

INGREDIENTS

- *1 cup peanut butter*
- *¾ cup golden caster sugar*
- *¼ tsp fine table salt*
- *1 large egg*

DIRECTIONS

1. Preheat the oven to 320°F, line 2 large baking trays with parchment.
2. Mix the peanut butter, sugar, and salt in a large bowl with a wooden spoon. Add the egg and mix until it forms a dough.
3. Break off apricot-sized dough chunks and place them, well spaced apart on the prepared trays. Press the cookies down with the back side of a fork to lightly squash them.
4. Bake for 12 minutes, until paler in the middle and golden around the edges.
5. Cool for 10 minutes on the trays, then place to a wire rack and let them cool completely before serving.

SNICKERS COOKIE BARS

SERVINGS: 12 | PREP TIME: 10 min. | COOK TIME: 30 min.

CARBS: 36 g | FAT: 25 g | PROTEIN: 5 g | CALORIES: 387

INGREDIENTS

For the shortbread layer:
- ⅔ cup butter softened
- ¼ cup sugar
- 1¼ cup all-purpose flour
- ¼ tsp salt
- 1 tsp pure vanilla extract

For the caramel layer:
- 1 11-ounce bag of caramels
- ¼ cup heavy cream
- 1 cup dry roasted plain peanuts

For the chocolate layer:
- 12 ounces milk chocolate chips

DIRECTIONS

1. Preheat the oven to 350°F. Line a 9x9 inch baking dish with parchment paper.
2. Cream the ingredients for the shortbread – butter, flour, vanilla, sugar, and salt – with a mixer on medium speed until fully incorporated and crumbled. Press it into the bottom of the prepared baking dish and bake for 18-20 minutes until slightly golden. Remove from the oven and set aside.
3. Add the caramels and heavy cream to a microwave-safe bowl and heat for 2 minutes, stirring after every 30 seconds. Mix in the peanuts and pour the prepared mixture over the shortbread. Distribute the caramel evenly with the back side of a spoon. Let it cool for 30 minutes.
4. Heat the chocolate in a microwave-safe bowl for 30 seconds at a time until melted, stirring each time. Pour the chocolate over the caramel layer and spread it evenly. Let it cool to room temperature and put it in the fridge to harden completely.
5. Cut into squares and serve!

COOKIE DOUGH PIZZA

SERVINGS: 15 | PREP TIME: 15 min. | COOK TIME: 25 min.

CARBS: 55 g | FAT: 21 g | PROTEIN: 5 g | CALORIES: 432

INGREDIENTS

- ¾ cup butter, softened
- 1 cup golden caster sugar
- ¾ cup soft light brown sugar
- 2 medium eggs, beaten
- 2 tsp vanilla extract
- 2¾ cups self-raising flour
- 1 tsp salt
- 1⅛ cups chocolate chips
- 2 cups chocolate ice cream
- Toppings to taste

DIRECTIONS

1. Preheat the oven to 360°F.
2. Beat the sugars with the butter in a large bowl with an electric mixer at medium speed. Pour in the eggs and vanilla and beat until combined.
3. Sift in the flour and salt and fold until well combined. Add in the chocolate chips and mix until rippled throughout the dough.
4. Roll the dough into a big round cookie and place it onto a large baking sheet covered with parchment. If it's too soft, put it in the fridge for 30 minutes.
5. Bake for 25 mins until golden at the edges and slightly wobbly in the center. Leave to cool for 10 minutes before topping with chocolate ice cream or toppings of your choice.

TRIPLE CHOCOLATE BROWNIES

SERVINGS: 16 | PREP TIME: 10 min. | COOK TIME: 30 min.

CARBS: 25 g | FAT: 15 g | PROTEIN: 4 g | CALORIES: 233

INGREDIENTS

- 1⅛ cups dark chocolate
- ⅘ cup unsalted butter
- 3 large eggs
- 1½ cups caster sugar
- ¾ cup plain flour
- ¼ cup cocoa powder
- ⅔ cup white chocolate chips
- ⅔ cup milk chocolate chips
- ⅔ cup dark chocolate chips

DIRECTIONS

1. Preheat the oven to 360°F, cover a 9-inch square baking tray with parchment paper.
2. Melt the butter and dark chocolate in a microwave-safe bowl for 1-2 minutes until melted. Leave to cool to room temperature.
3. Whisk the eggs and the caster sugar with an electric mixer for 2-3 minutes or so until the mixture becomes pale and has doubled in size.
4. Once done, pour the cooled chocolate mixture over the eggs and fold it very carefully to avoid knocking out the air.
5. Once completely combined, sift the cocoa powder and flour on top of the chocolate mix and then carefully fold again.
6. Fold through the rest of the chocolate chips and pour it into the prepared tray. Bake for 25-30 minutes.
7. Let it completely cool in the tin. Slice and serve.

CHERRY CHOCOLATE BROWNIES

SERVINGS: 20 | PREP TIME: 30 min. | COOK TIME: 40 min.

CARBS: 34 g | FAT: 17 g | PROTEIN: 3 g | CALORIES: 310

INGREDIENTS

- *1 cup unsalted butter, softened at room temperature, plus extra for greasing*
- *1 Tbsp instant coffee powder*
- *1⅖ cups light brown soft sugar*
- *4 medium eggs*
- *½ cup cocoa powder*
- *¾ cup self-raising flour*
- *1 tsp cherry essence (optional)*
- *¼ cup fresh cherries, chopped*

For the decorating:
- *1½ cup dark chocolate*
- *20 glazed cherries*
- *2 Tbsp powdered sugar*

DIRECTIONS

1. Grease a 12x8-inch cake tin and line with parchment paper. Preheat the oven to 360°F.
2. Mix the coffee with 2 Tbsp boiling water and set aside to cool.
3. Cream the butter and sugar for 5 minutes with an electric mixer on medium speed until light and fluffy. Add the eggs – one at a time – incorporating well after each egg.
4. In another bowl, mix the cocoa powder and flour. Add the essence and cooled coffee to the prepared butter mixture, then add the flour and mix. Mix well and fold in the chopped cherries. Spoon the batter into the lined tin, smooth the top with the back side of a spoon.
5. Bake for 30 minutes or so until a toothpick inserted into the center comes out clean. Let it cool in the tin.
6. Once completely cooled, melt the chocolate in the microwave, then spread over the top of the brownie in an even layer.
7. Cut it into 20 squares, dust the top with powdered sugar and place glazed cherries on top of each brownie.

BASIC CUPCAKES AND ICING

SERVINGS: 12 | PREP TIME: 10 min. | COOK TIME: 20 min.

CARBS: 18 g | FAT: 10 g | PROTEIN: 2 g | CALORIES: 173

INGREDIENTS

For the cupcakes:
- *½ cup butter softened/margarine*
- *125g caster sugar*
- *125g self-raising flour*
- *2 large eggs, beaten*
- *1 tsp vanilla extract*
  For the icing:
- *½ cup unsalted butter, softened*
- *½ tsp vanilla extract*
- *2 cups confectioners' sugar, sifted*
- *2 Tbsp milk*

DIRECTIONS

1. Preheat the oven to 360°F.
2. Cream the butter and sugar for the cupcakes in a bowl for 5 minutes with a mixer on medium speed. Stir in the beaten eggs and vanilla extract. Sift in the flour. Mix it until just combined. Divide the mixture between the cupcake cases, filling them halfway. Bake in the oven for 20 minutes.
3. The cupcakes are cooked once they have risen and are golden brown. A toothpick inserted in the middle of the cupcake must come out clean.
4. Cream the butter for the filling with a mixer until fluffy and smooth. Gradually add in the confectioners' sugar and beat until fully incorporated. Beat in the vanilla extract.
5. Pour in the milk and beat for 3-4 more minutes. Continue beating until you get the desired thickness.

UNICORN CUPCAKES

SERVINGS: 12 | PREP TIME: 10 min. | COOK TIME: 10 min.

CARBS: 24 g | FAT: 8 g | PROTEIN: 4 g | CALORIES: 201

INGREDIENTS

- *12 cupcakes (from Basic Cupcakes and Icing recipe)*

For the icing:
- *1 cup butter, softened*
- *3 cups icing sugar*
- *2 tsp vanilla*
- *¼ cup milk*

For the decorating:
- *White Fondant, as much as needed*
- *12 colorful cake candles*
- *Edible glitter and sprinkles*
- *Pink food coloring gel, as much as needed*

DIRECTIONS

1. To make unicorn ears, roll the fondant out (5-mm thick), and cut strips about 2 cm wide with a knife. Cut the strips into triangles. Mix 2 drops of pink food coloring with water. Paint the inside of the triangles with a paintbrush. Squeeze together the bottom corners of the triangles, to create an ear shape. Leave the ears for 1-2 hours to harden.
2. Beat the butter with an electric mixer for 2-3 minutes or so until it is white. Add the icing sugar and milk, alternate adding sugar and milk.
3. Fill your piping bag with icing. Ice your cupcakes with swirls.
4. Once the ears harden, top each cupcake with two ears and a candle as a unicorn horn. Add sprinkles on top and serve!

APPLE MUFFINS

SERVINGS: 18 | PREP TIME: 10 min. | COOK TIME: 20 min.

CARBS: 39 g | FAT: 13 g | PROTEIN: 2 g | CALORIES: 280

INGREDIENTS

- *1½ cups sugar*
- *2 eggs*
- *1 cup oil*
- *1 Tbsp vanilla*
- *3 cups flour*
- *1 tsp salt*
- *1 tsp baking soda*
- *1 tsp cinnamon*
- *3 cups peeled, cored, diced apples*
- *½ cup brown sugar for topping*

DIRECTIONS

1. Preheat the oven to 350°F, line your muffin pan with 18 paper liners.
2. Cream the sugar, oil, eggs, and vanilla with a mixer in a bowl until it is a pale-yellow color.
3. In another bowl, whisk the flour, baking soda, ground cinnamon, and salt. Add the dry mixture to creamed egg mixture and mix until well combined. The batter will have a texture similar to cookie dough. Mix in the diced apples.
4. Fill the paper liners about ¾ of the way full. Sprinkle each top with brown sugar.
5. Bake for 20-24 minutes.
6. Let the muffins cool for 10-15 minutes before serving.

CHRISTMAS EVE CUPCAKES

SERVINGS: 12 | PREP TIME: 10 min. | COOK TIME: 15 min.

CARBS: 63 g | FAT: 28 g | PROTEIN: 3 g | CALORIES: 510

INGREDIENTS

For the cupcakes:
- ⅔ cup caster sugar
- 3 medium eggs free range
- ⅔ cup unsalted butter at room temperature
- 1 cup self-raising flour

For the icing:
- 1 cup unsalted butter
- 4 cups icing sugar, sieved
- 2-3 drops green gel food coloring
- Christmas themed sprinkles

DIRECTIONS

1. Preheat oven to 360°F.
2. Put 12 cupcakes cases into your tin ready.
3. Cream the butter with the sugar with an electric mixer until pale, light, and fluffy. Beat in the eggs – one at a time – mixing well after each egg. Mix in the flour. Spoon equal amounts of prepared mixture into the cupcake cases.
4. Bake for 15 minutes. The cupcakes should be golden and a little bouncy to touch.
5. To make the icing beat your butter until light, pale, and fluffy. Beat in the icing sugar.
6. Let the cupcakes cool to room temperature. Once they have cooled, pipe Christmas trees on top. Look for the piping technique in the Baking Techniques and Skills subchapter.
7. Sprinkle on some sprinkles and serve!

BLUEBERRY MUFFINS

SERVINGS: 8 | PREP TIME: 1 h. | COOK TIME: 30 min.

CARBS: 20 g | FAT: 13 g | PROTEIN: 3 g | CALORIES: 214

INGREDIENTS

- *4 oz plain flour*
- *4 oz butter, softened*
- *2½ oz caster sugar*
- *2 free-range eggs*
- *1½ tsp baking powder*
- *4½ oz blueberries*
- *1 pinch grated nutmeg*

DIRECTIONS

1. Cream the sugar and butter, next gradually add the eggs while mixing for three minutes. Add the flour, baking powder, and nutmeg. Stir to combine, and leave in the fridge overnight.
2. When it's done, preheat the oven to 390°F.
3. Add a spoonful of mixture into each muffin case, filling them just over halfway. Drop about eight blueberries into each muffin.
4. Bake for 21 minutes or so until the tops are golden.
5. Let them cool to warm before serving.

RAINBOW CUPCAKES

SERVINGS: 24 | PREP TIME: 30 min. | COOK TIME: 30 min.

CARBS: 28 g | FAT: 13 g | PROTEIN: 5 g | CALORIES: 230

INGREDIENTS

- *1 cup butter, softened*
- *2⅓ cups sugar*
- *5 egg whites*
- *1 Tbsp vanilla*
- *3 cups flour*
- *4 tsp baking powder*
- *½ tsp salt*
- *1½ cups milk, warmed for 30 sec in the microwave to bring to room temp*
- *Rainbow colors Gel food coloring*
- *¾ of 2 lb piping bag of vanilla frosting (Basic Cupcakes and Icing recipe)*

DIRECTIONS

1. Preheat the oven to 350°F. Prepare your cupcake cases.
2. Cream the sugar and butter with a mixer for 2-3 minutes until light in color. Mix in the egg whites and vanilla until fully combined.
3. Mix the flour, baking powder, and salt in another bowl. Then add the flour mixture and milk to the butter mixture alternating 1 cup flour and ½ cup milk at a time.
4. Divide the prepared batter between six different bowls. Color each bowl with gel food coloring in rainbow colors. Mix until the colors are mixed in. You can also add 2-3 drops of blue food coloring to your icing and barely mix it to get icing like the photo.
5. Using a small spoon, spoon just under a Tbsp of batter into each cup in this order: purple, blue, green, yellow, then orange, and red. Or in your preferred order. Bake for 18-20 minutes. Let them cool before icing them.
6. Pipe icing onto the top of the cooled cupcakes and sprinkle with decorations if desired. Serve!

TWILIGHT SKY CUPCAKES

SERVINGS: 24 | PREP TIME: 5 min. | COOK TIME: 15 min.

CARBS: 27 g | FAT: 16 g | PROTEIN: 6 g | CALORIES: 251

INGREDIENTS

- *24 cupcakes, cooled completely and 2 tubs white icing (Basic Cupcakes and Icing recipe)*
- *2-3 drops violet food coloring*
- *2-3 drops blue food coloring*
- *2-3 drops black food coloring*
- *Silver sprinkles and stars for decorating*
- *Wilton Silver Cake Sequins*

DIRECTIONS

1. Divide 1 tub of icing into four bowls and color the three bowls with black, blue, and violet food coloring.
2. When filling the piping bag, use a knife to spread the icing along the side of the bag (a large star tip fitted).
3. Pipe onto the 12 cupcakes.
4. Sprinkle with silver decorations and top each cupcake with a star.
5. Serve and enjoy your galaxy cupcakes.

MINI ICED DONUTS

SERVINGS: 12 | PREP TIME: 15 min. | COOK TIME: 20 min.

CARBS: 38 g | FAT: 6 g | PROTEIN: 2 g | CALORIES: 211

INGREDIENTS

For the donuts:
- *⅓ cup unsalted butter, softened*
- *3¾ oz caster sugar*
- *1 egg*
- *3 ¾ fl oz milk*
- *1 tsp vanilla extract*
- *2 tsp baking powder*
- *1⅓ cups plain white flour*

For the glaze:
- *6 oz icing sugar*
- *2 tsp vanilla extract*
- *4 tsp water*
- *Violet and green food coloring gel*

For the chocolate glaze:
- *½ cup melted chocolate*
- *2 Tbsp unsalted butter*
- *2 tsp honey*
- *2 tsp water*

DIRECTIONS

1. Preheat the oven to 320°F. Grease a mini donut tray.
2. Mix the butter and sugar with a mixer for 2-3 minutes in a large bowl until light and fluffy. Gradually add in the egg, vanilla, and milk. Next, fold in the flour, baking powder, and a pinch of salt. Spoon the mixture evenly into the greased tin and bake for 10 minutes until golden and risen. Let the donuts cool.
3. To make the glaze, mix icing sugar, vanilla extract, and water in a bowl until smooth. Divide it between 3 small bowls. Add 2-3 drops of green food coloring gel to one bowl, and the violet to another bowl. Mix well. You can add more or less gel to reach the desired color.
4. To make the chocolate glaze, add butter, chocolate, honey, and water to another bowl. Melt in the microwave – for 20 seconds at a time – stirring after each time until fully melted and smooth.
5. To glaze, dip each donut in icing to cover a third of the way down. Leave them to sit for 5-10 minutes and serve.

SUGAR COOKIE DONUTS

SERVINGS: 20 | PREP TIME: 15 min. | COOK TIME: 5 min.

CARBS: 20 g | FAT: 11 g | PROTEIN: 2 g | CALORIES: 190

INGREDIENTS

For the donuts:
- *2 cups dry sugar cookie mix*
- *¼ tsp baking soda*
- *1 egg, beaten*
- *1 Tbsp butter, melted*
- *1 Tbsp vegetable oil*
- *½ cup milk*
- *1 Tbsp vinegar*

For the glaze:
- *1 cup powdered sugar*
- *2 Tbsp milk*
- *1 tsp vegetable shortening*
- *1 drop red food coloring*

DIRECTIONS

1. Preheat the oven to 350°F. Grease a donut tray with butter.
2. Mix the milk and vinegar and don't worry when it curdles.
3. Mix the baking soda and dry sugar mix in a bowl. Then add the egg, oil, butter, and curdled milk. Mix until well blended.
4. Fill each donut reservoir evenly with 2 Tbsp batter.
5. Bake for 15-17 minutes or so until a toothpick inserted in the center of the donut comes out clean. Place donuts on a cooling rack.
6. Whisk the powdered sugar, milk, shortening, and food coloring in a small bowl until smooth.
7. Once the donuts have cooled, dip the top of each donut in the glaze, add sprinkles, and put it back on the cooling rack to let the glaze dry.

CINNAMON BAKED DONUTS

SERVINGS: 12 | PREP TIME: 35 min. | COOK TIME: 15 min.

CARBS: 70 g | FAT: 3 g | PROTEIN: 4 g | CALORIES: 290

INGREDIENTS

For the donuts:
- 2 cups all-purpose flour
- 1½ cups sugar
- 2 tsp baking powder
- 1 tsp ground cinnamon
- ½ tsp ground nutmeg
- ½ tsp kosher salt
- 1 extra-large egg, lightly beaten
- 1¼ cups whole milk
- 2 Tbsp unsalted butter, melted
- 2 tsp pure vanilla extract

For the topping:
- 8 Tbsp (1 stick) unsalted butter
- ½ cup sugar
- ½ tsp ground cinnamon

DIRECTIONS

1. Preheat the oven to 350°F. Spray two donut pans well.
2. Sift the flour, sugar, baking powder, cinnamon, nutmeg, and salt in one large bowl.
3. Whisk the egg, melted butter, milk, and vanilla in a small bowl. Stir the wet mixture into dry one until combined.
4. Spoon the batter into the donut pans, filling each one a bit more than ¾ full. Bake for 17 minutes and check if it's ready – a toothpick should come out clean. Let them cool for 5 minutes and tip the cooked donuts on a sheet pan.
5. Meanwhile, melt butter in a sauté pan for the topping. Mix the cinnamon and sugar in a bowl. Dip each donut in the butter and then in the cinnamon-sugar mixture on one side and serve.

CHOCOLATE SPRINKLE DONUTS

SERVINGS: 6 | PREP TIME: 5 min. | COOK TIME: 10 min.

CARBS: 64 g | FAT: 23 g | PROTEIN: 5 g | CALORIES: 473

INGREDIENTS

For the donuts:
- 1 cup flour
- ½ cup sugar
- ¼ cup cocoa powder
- ½ tsp baking soda
- ½ tsp espresso powder
- ½ tsp vanilla extract
- 1 egg
- 6 Tbsp sour cream
- ¼ cup milk
- ¼ cup vegetable oil

For the frosting:
- ½ cup white sugar
- 3 Tbsp butter
- 3 Tbsp milk
- ⅓ cup semi-sweet chocolate chips
- ¼ cup sprinkles

DIRECTIONS

1. Preheat the oven to 375°F.
2. Mix the flour, sugar, baking soda, cocoa, and espresso powder in a mixing bowl.
3. Beat the vanilla, egg, milk, sour cream, and oil in a small bowl.
4. Stir the wet components into the dry until just combined. Spoon the prepared batter evenly in a greased donut pan.
5. Bake for 8 minutes or so until the tops spring back when touched. Let the donuts cool before topping them.
6. Add the butter, sugar, and milk to a saucepan and bring to a boil over a medium heat. Boil for 1 minute and turn off.
7. Stir in the chocolate chips and stir until the chocolate has completely melted. Use the frosting immediately once it has cooked.
8. Dip the tops of the donuts into the frosting and place them on a cooling rack.
9. Top with sprinkles and let them sit for 10 minutes before serving.

STRAWBERRY LEMON DONUTS

SERVINGS: 6-7 | PREP TIME: 5 min. | COOK TIME: 12 min.

CARBS: 32 g | FAT: 8 g | PROTEIN: 3 g | CALORIES: 210

INGREDIENTS

For the donuts:
- ¼ cup milk
- 2 tsp lemon juice
- ¼ tsp vanilla
- ⅓ cup honey
- 3½ Tbsp butter, melted
- 2 eggs
- 1 cup flour
- 1 tsp lemon zest
- ¼ tsp salt
- 1 tsp baking powder
- ½ cup finely diced strawberries

For the glaze:
- 1 cup powdered sugar
- 2 Tbsp lemon juice
- 1 tsp lemon zest very well
- 1-3 tsp milk (only if necessary)

DIRECTIONS

1. Preheat the oven to 350°F, grease a pan for the donuts.
2. Mix the lemon juice, milk, melted butter, vanilla, honey, and eggs in a small bowl. Whisk well to combine and set aside.
3. Mix the lemon zest, flour, salt, and baking powder in another bowl.
4. Stir the wet ingredients into the dry ones until just combined.
5. Carefully fold in the strawberries.
6. Portion the dough into the prepared donut pan, approximately 3½ Tbsp per donut.
7. Bake for 13-16 minutes until risen and golden.
8. Let them chill for 5 minutes in the pan, then transfer to a cooling rack and let them cool completely.
9. Whisk the lemon juice and zest with powdered sugar for the glaze in a small bowl. If you think it's too thick, thin by adding milk, 1 tsp at a time.
10. Dunk the cooled donuts in the lemon glaze and serve.

BIRTHDAY CAKE

SERVINGS: 8 | PREP TIME: 20 min. | COOK TIME: 25 min.

CARBS: 45 g | FAT: 28 g | PROTEIN: 5 g | CALORIES: 448

INGREDIENTS

For the cake:
- *1 cup butter, at room temperature*
- *1 cup golden caster sugar*
- *4 large eggs*
- *1¾ cup self-raising flour*
- *3 Tbsp whole milk*
- *1 tsp vanilla extract*
- *2 Tbsp cocoa powder*

For the icing:
- *⅔ cup butter, very soft*
- *2½ cup icing sugar, sifted*

DIRECTIONS

1. Preheat the oven to 360°F. Grease two 8-inch round loose-based cake tins and, using baking parchment, line the bases.
2. Beat the butter and sugar in a mixer, then gradually add the eggs – one at a time – mixing well after each one. Fold in the flour, milk, and vanilla until you get a smooth mixture.
3. Divide the prepared mixture between two bowls. Sift the cocoa powder into one bowl. Scrape the vanilla batter into one tin and the chocolate batter into another and level the tops.
4. Bake for 20-25 mins or so until a toothpick comes out clean. Let them cool for 5 minutes in the tin and then take out onto a wire rack to cool completely.
5. Beat the butter with a mixer for 2 minutes and then start adding icing sugar – a little at a time – beating enough to get a smooth icing after each addition.
6. Sandwich the two cooked cakes together with the prepared icing and spread the rest of the icing on top using a palette knife. Decorate with candies, cookies, or anything you want.

BANANA CAKE

SERVINGS: 12 | PREP TIME: 15 min. | COOK TIME: 1 h. 5 min.

CARBS: 62 g | FAT: 18 g | PROTEIN: 5 g | CALORIES: 427

INGREDIENTS

For the cake:
- *1 cup plain flour*
- *2½ tsp baking powder*
- *1 tsp cinnamon*
- *½ tsp ground ginger*
- *1½ cup golden caster sugar*
- *½ cup unsalted butter, very soft*
- *3 large eggs*
- *½ cup soured cream*
- *¼ tsp salt*

For the topping:
- *⅓ cup unsalted butter, more for greasing*
- *¾ cup light muscovado sugar*
- *½ tsp vanilla bean paste*
- *4 large bananas*

DIRECTIONS

1. Heat the oven to 360°F and lightly grease a deep 9-inch round cake tin, and line the base with baking parchment.
2. To make the topping, add butter and sugar to a saucepan and cook over a medium heat until melted and combined. Add the vanilla and mix well. Pour into the cake tin and spread it in one layer. Cut the bananas in half lengthways and arrange them on top of the caramel, cut-side down.
3. Add all of the cake components to a large bowl. Beat with a mixer for 3-4 minutes or so on low speed until the batter is smooth and mixed well. Pour the batter on top of the bananas, level it out with a spatula. Bake for 1 hour until a toothpick inserted in the center of the cake comes out clean. If the cake becomes too dark, cover it with foil after 45 minutes of baking.
4. Take out of the oven and let it cool for 10 minutes before turning out onto a plate and then serve warm!

CHOCOLATE CHEESECAKE

SERVINGS: 10 | PREP TIME: 25 min. | COOK TIME: 2 h.

CARBS: 25 g | FAT: 20 g | PROTEIN: 3 g | CALORIES: 296

INGREDIENTS

For the base:
- 5.3 oz digestive biscuits
- 1 Tbsp caster sugar
- 3 Tbsp butter, melted, plus extra for the tin

For the cheesecake:
- 1 cup dark chocolate
- ½ cup double cream
- 2 tsp cocoa powder
- ¾ cup full-fat cream cheese
- ½ cup caster sugar

DIRECTIONS

1. To make the base, crush the biscuits with a blitz in a food processor. Mix the crushed cookies, sugar, and butter in a bowl and mix well to combine. Butter and line a 7-inch springform tin. Spread the biscuit mixture on the bottom, pushing it down with the back of a spoon. Put in the fridge for 30 minutes to chill it.

2. Meanwhile, melt the chocolate in the microwave in short bursts, and let it cool for 2 minutes.

3. Whip the cream with an electric whisk in a large bowl until soft peaks start to form, then fold in the cocoa powder. Beat the sugar and cream cheese in another bowl, then fold in the cream mixture and chilled chocolate.

4. Spoon the prepared mixture over the chilled biscuit base, leveling it out with the back side of the spoon. Put in the freezer for 1 hour.

5. Once ready to serve, remove the cake from the tin and let it warm to room temperature for 20 minutes before serving.

CARROT CAKE

SERVINGS: 10-12 | PREP TIME: 15 min. | COOK TIME: 1 h. 15 min.

CARBS: 43 g | FAT: 23 g | PROTEIN: 5 g | CALORIES: 406

INGREDIENTS

For the cake:
- *Butter, for greasing*
- *⅔ cup raisins*
- *4 Tbsp sweet orange juice*
- *3 large eggs*
- *¾ cup sunflower oil*
- *1 cup light muscovado sugar*
- *2 tsp ground cinnamon*
- *1¾ cup self-raising flour*
- *½ tsp baking powder*
- *½ tsp bicarbonate of soda*
- *¼ cup desiccated coconut*
- *1 cup walnut pieces*
- *1 cup carrot, roughly grated + 2 Tbsp for topping*

For the icing:
- *1¼ cup low-fat cream cheese*
- *½ cup icing sugar*
- *1 tsp vanilla extract*

DIRECTIONS

1. Preheat the oven to 360°F. Grease a 9-inch round, loose-bottomed cake tin with butter. Line the base with a circle of baking paper.
2. Pour the orange juice into a saucepan. Add the raisins to the pan with the orange juice and bring to a boil. Simmer gently for 2 minutes until the raisins have absorbed all of the liquid. Set aside.
3. Whisk the eggs, oil, and sugar in a bowl with an electric whisk for 3 minutes until it becomes creamy.
4. Sift in the cinnamon, baking powder, flour, and soda over the egg mixture, and fold in with the walnuts, coconut, raisins, and carrot.
5. Spoon the batter into the tin and bake for 45 minutes until a toothpick pushed into the cake's center comes out clean. Let it cool for 15 minutes, then take out of the tin and transfer to a wire rack to cool completely.
6. Beat all ingredients for the icing in a bowl until smooth and creamy. Spread the prepared icing over top and sides of the cake and sprinkle with grated carrot and extra walnuts.

ARCTIC CAKE

SERVINGS: 10 | PREP TIME: 25 min. | COOK TIME: 35 min.

CARBS: 25 g | FAT: 5 g | PROTEIN: 2 g | CALORIES: 150

INGREDIENTS

- *Cooking spray, for pan*
- *Flour, for dusting*
- *1 vanilla cake (from <u>Birthday Cake</u> recipe)*
- *1 can vanilla frosting*
- *1 cake donut, halved*
- *1 10-oz. bag marshmallows*
- *1 cup mini marshmallows*
- *Powdered sugar, for sifting*

DIRECTIONS

1. Preheat the oven to 350°F. Grease an 8-inch cake pan and an 8-inch oven-safe bowl (it should have a completely rounded bottom). Dust with flour, tapping out the excess.
2. Pour a little more than half of the batter into a bowl, then pour the rest of the batter into the round pan. Bake for 25 minutes until a toothpick comes out clean from the center. Bake the cake in the bowl for 10 minutes longer. Invert both cakes onto a cooling rack to let them cool completely.
3. Spread the frosting over the whole surface of the bowl cake on top, larger side on the bottom. Cover the whole cake with the rest of the vanilla frosting.
4. Glue donut halves together with frosting and press onto the front bottom of the cake to create a doorway. Cover with frosting.
5. Starting from the bottom of the cake, press marshmallows into the frosting, packing them closely in even rows until you reach the top of the cake. Decorate the doorway with marshmallows too.
6. Sift powdered sugar on top and serve!

UNICORN CHEESECAKE

SERVINGS: 8 | PREP TIME: 25 min. | COOK TIME: 6 h. 25 min.

CARBS: 21 g | FAT: 16 g | PROTEIN: 3 g | CALORIES: 257

INGREDIENTS

- *16 oz cream cheese, softened*
- *2 tsp vanilla extract*
- *1 cup sugar*
- *2 cups heavy cream*
- *1 crust (from <u>Chocolate Cheesecake</u> recipe)*
- *Coconut flakes, for decorating*
- *Blue, pink, green, yellow, and purple food coloring*
- *Whipped cream, for serving*

DIRECTIONS

1. Beat the cream cheese and sugar using an electric mixer in a large bowl for 3 minutes until smooth and fluffy.
2. Add the heavy cream and beat for 2-3 minutes until stiff peaks start to form. Add the vanilla and beat to combine.
3. Divide the mixture evenly among 5 bowls and add a few drops of a different food coloring to each bowl. Stir to combine.
4. Add spoonfuls of the prepared cheesecake mixtures to the crust, alternating colors until all mixture is gone.
5. Top the edges with a little whipped cream and sprinkles.
6. Set in the fridge for 8 hours until the cheesecake is firm and sliceable.
7. Serve with more whipped cream.

PIE CRUST

SERVINGS: 2 | PREP TIME: 3 h. 15 min. | COOK TIME: 15-20 min.

CARBS: 22 g | FAT: 9 g | PROTEIN: 2 g | CALORIES: 177

INGREDIENTS

- *2½ cups all-purpose flour*
- *2 tsp sugar*
- *½ cup cold vegetable shortening*
  1 tsp salt
- *½ cup ice water*
- *½ cup cold unsalted butter*
  cubed, cut into a few pieces

DIRECTIONS

1. Whisk the sugar, salt, and flour in a bowl until combined. Add the butter and shortening – with a fork, cut them into the flour mixture until small pea-sized crumbs form.
2. Gradually add the ice water – 1 Tbsp at a time – and carefully mix it in until it starts to come together.
3. Turn the dough out onto a dusted table, shape a ball. Cut in half and flatten the halves into two discs. Cover each tightly, using plastic wrap, and put in the fridge for 1 hour.
4. Roll the dough out to 12-inches in diameter, transfer it to a 9-inch pie plate, trim excess dough to fit it, and decorate the edges. Line the pie dough with baking parchment, covering all sides and the bottom, then fill with pie weights. Bake for 15 minutes at 400°F with the pie weights. Remove from the oven, remove the paper and weights. Using a fork, prick the whole of the bottom of the crust.
5. Put back in the oven and bake for another 16-20 minutes until golden brown and cooked through.

SOUTHERN BUTTERMILK PIE

SERVINGS: 24 | PREP TIME: 3 h. | COOK TIME: 15 min.

CARBS: 21 g | FAT: 4 g | PROTEIN: 1 g | CALORIES: 124

INGREDIENTS

- *1 ½ cups sugar*
- *3 Tbsp all-purpose flour*
- *3 large eggs*
- *1 cup buttermilk*
- *½ cup butter, melted*
- *1 Tbsp lemon zest*
- *3 Tbsp lemon juice*
- *1 tsp vanilla extract*
- *1 pie crust (Pie Crust recipe)*
- *Garnishes: fresh berries, whipped cream, fresh mint*

DIRECTIONS

1. Preheat the oven to 350°F.
2. Whisk the sugar and flour in a large bowl. Whisk the eggs, buttermilk, butter, vanilla, lemon zest, and juice into the flour mixture until well combined. Pour the prepared mixture into the pie crust.
3. Bake for 35-45 minutes until almost set, covering the edges with foil after 15 minutes of baking.
4. Take out of the oven and transfer the pie to a wire rack to cool completely before serving.

MIXED FRUIT TART

SERVINGS: 8 | PREP TIME: 25 min. | COOK TIME: 2 h.

CARBS: 31 g | FAT: 36 g | PROTEIN: 5 g | CALORIES: 471

INGREDIENTS

- *220g plain flour, + extra for dusting*
- *1 Tbsp golden caster sugar*
- *110g unsalted butter, chilled and diced*
- *3 Tbsp cold water*
- *1 pinch of salt*
- *1 large egg yolk*
- *½ cup mascarpone*
- *1 cup double cream*
- *1 tsp vanilla bean paste*
- *1 Tbsp icing sugar*
- *1½ cup fruit of choice*

DIRECTIONS

1. Preheat the oven to 360°F.
2. Add the flour, sugar, and salt to the bowl of a food processor, pulse to combine. Add the butter and pulse more until it resembles coarse breadcrumbs. Add the egg yolk and water, and pulse until the mixture just comes together. Transfer the dough onto a work surface and bring it into a combined dough. Wrap, using plastic wrap, and chill for 2 hours.
3. Flour your work surface, roll out the dough, and line a 9-inch tart tin with rolled-out pastry. Trim off the excess and chill for 30 minutes.
4. Remove from the fridge and prick the pastry shell with a fork and line with baking parchment. Fill with pie weights and bake in the oven for 20 minutes. Remove the parchment and weights, put the pastry back in the oven for 12-14 more minutes. Take out of tin and place on a wire rack to cool completely.
5. Meanwhile, whisk the cream, mascarpone, vanilla, and icing sugar in a large bowl until it starts to hold soft peaks. Spread the prepared filling into the cooled pastry case in one layer. Decorate with fresh fruit and serve!

WHIPPED CREAM LIME PIE

SERVINGS: 8 | PREP TIME: 1 d. | COOK TIME: 15 min.

CARBS: 38 g | FAT: 28 g | PROTEIN: 5 g | CALORIES: 427

INGREDIENTS

- 2 cups graham cracker crumbs
- ½ cup granulated sugar
- ½ cup salted butter, melted, + more for greasing dish
- 1 14-oz. can sweetened condensed milk
- ½ cup key lime juice
- 1 Tbsp lime zest + more, for topping
- 3 cups whipped cream, divided
- 1 lime, thinly sliced

DIRECTIONS

1. Preheat the oven to 325°F. Mix the cracker crumbs, butter, and sugar in a bowl to combine. Press the crumb mixture firmly into a lightly greased 9-inch pie tin. Bake until the crust is golden brown, about 18-20 minutes. Remove from the oven, and allow to cool completely on a wire rack, about 30 minutes.
2. Mix the milk, lime juice, and zest in a large bowl until completely combined. Fold in 2 cups of whipped cream. Spread the mixture into the cooled pie crust, and chill in the fridge overnight.
3. Fill a piping bag with 1 cup whipped cream, and decorate your pie with swirls of whipped cream. Top with lime slices and sprinkle with lime zest over the whipped cream.

MINI LEMON TARTS

SERVINGS: 6 | PREP TIME: 20 min. | COOK TIME: 30 min.

CARBS: 42 g | FAT: 29 g | PROTEIN: 8 g | CALORIES: 449

INGREDIENTS

For the tarts:
- ½ cup (1 stick) unsalted butter
- ¼ cup sugar
- 1 cup all-purpose flour
- ¼ tsp fine sea salt
- ½ tsp vanilla extract
- 1 cup lemon curd
- Whipped cream, to taste
- Berries of choice, if desired

For the lemon curd:
- 1 Tbsp lemon zest
- ¾ cup fresh lemon juice
- ½ cup sugar
- ¼ tsp fine sea salt
- 3 large eggs + 4 large egg yolks
- 4 Tbsp unsalted butter, cubed

DIRECTIONS

1. Cream the sugar and butter for 2-3 minutes with an electric mixer on medium in a bowl. Stir in the vanilla. Add the flour and salt and mix well. Put in the fridge for 30 minutes.
2. Whisk the eggs and egg yolks well in a bowl. Set aside.
3. Heat the lemon juice and zest, sugar, and salt in a small saucepan over a medium heat until the sugar has dissolved. Turn off the heat. Slowly scoop ½ cup of prepared sugar mixture into prepared eggs while whisking.
4. While whisking, pour the egg mixture into the pan on the stove. Turn the heat back on and cook for 5 minutes on low, whisking, until the mixture has thickened. Don't stop whisking or it will start to curdle!
5. Turn off the heat and mix in the butter until it's fully mixed in. Strain the curd by pushing it through a fine-mesh strainer. (Optional)
6. Cover the lemon curd with plastic wrap and chill until ready to use.
7. Preheat the oven to 300°F.
8. Remove the dough from the fridge and press into mini tart pans. Place on a sheet and bake for 10-15 minutes until lightly golden. Let them cool to room temperature.
9. Fill each tart crust with the prepared lemon curd. Decorate with berries and whipped cream if desired.

BERRY PIE

SERVINGS: 8 | PREP TIME: 10 min. | COOK TIME: 45 min.

CARBS: 40 g | FAT: 11 g | PROTEIN: 2 g | CALORIES: 271

INGREDIENTS

- *2 pie crusts (Pie Crust recipe)*
- *4 cups frozen berries of choice*
- *1 cup sugar*
- *¼ cup cornstarch*
- *¼ tsp salt*

DIRECTIONS

1. Preheat the oven to 375°F.
2. Let the berries thaw in a large bowl. Once thawed, do not rinse the berries or juice.
3. Mix the cornstarch, sugar, and salt in another bowl. Pour over the thawed berries and mix well to combine. It should become thick.
4. Place one pie dough crust in the bottom of a greased 9-inch pie dish.
5. Spread the berry mixture evenly in the prepared pie crust.
6. Top the pie with the second crust. Cut slits in the top crust. Squeeze the edges of the pie around the top of your index finger with your thumb and other index finger until you squeeze it completely.
7. Bake for 45-55 minutes until the crusts are golden brown.
8. Take out of the oven and let the pie cool for 10-15 minutes before serving.

CHEESY CHICKEN CASSEROLE

SERVINGS: 6 | PREP TIME: 30 min. | COOK TIME: 30 min.

CARBS: 32 g | FAT: 39 g | PROTEIN: 40 g | CALORIES: 649

INGREDIENTS

- 3 cups shell noodles uncooked
- 3 Tbsp butter
- ⅓ cup red bell pepper diced
- 1 onion finely diced
- ½ tsp seasoning salt
- 1 tsp chili powder
- 10 ¾ oz chicken cream soup
- 1 ⅓ cups milk
- 3 cups sharp Cheddar cheese shredded, divided
- ⅓ cup Parmesan cheese shredded
- ½ cup green peas
- 3 cups cooked chicken

DIRECTIONS

1. Preheat the oven to 375°F.
2. Cook the shells al dente following the package directions.
3. Heat the butter in a pan over a medium-high heat.
4. Once melted, add the onion and pepper, and cook for 5 minutes. Season with salt and chili powder.
5. Mix the soup, cooked onions and pepper, milk, parmesan, and 2 cups Cheddar in a large bowl. Mix well to combine. Stir in the chicken, cooked pasta, and green peas.
6. Spread into a 9x13-inch casserole dish. Top with the rest of the Cheddar cheese.
7. Bake for 30-35 minutes until bubbling and hot.
8. Let it sit for 12 minutes and serve.

VEGETABLE CASSEROLE

SERVINGS: 00 | PREP TIME: 40 min. | COOK TIME: 8 h. 35 min.

CARBS: 9 g | FAT: 10 g | PROTEIN: 3 g | CALORIES: 144

INGREDIENTS

- ¾ lb uncooked sausage, casings removed
- 2 bell peppers, diced
- 1 cup sliced mushrooms
- 1 cup fresh spinach
- ½ yellow onion, diced
- 1 tsp minced garlic
- Salt and black pepper, to taste
- 4 slices bread you like, ripped in pieces
- 10 large eggs
- ½ cup milk
- ½ cup shredded cheese

DIRECTIONS

1. Heat a skillet over a medium heat with oil. Add the sausage to the skillet and break it up with a spatula. Add in the rosemary and brown the sausage for 6-7 minutes. Set aside.
2. At the same time, set a second skillet over a medium heat and drizzle with olive oil. Add the peppers, mushrooms, spinach, onion, garlic, salt, and pepper. Cook for 6-8 minutes, stirring. Set aside.
3. Grease a 9x13-inch baking pan. Place bread pieces in the pan in an even layer.
4. Whisk the eggs, milk, and ¼ cup cheese in a large bowl. Pour ½ egg mixture over bread. Top with sausage and vegetables, then with the rest of the egg mixture and ¼ cup cheese. Season with salt and pepper to taste.
5. Cover, using plastic wrap, and put in the fridge for 2 hours. Let it come to room temperature when ready to bake.
6. Preheat the oven to 375°F.
7. Bake for 45-50 minutes, uncovered, until the top is golden and the edges are crisp. Let it cool for 10 minutes, slice, and serve.

MASHED POTATO CASSEROLE

SERVINGS: 12 | PREP TIME: 30 min. | COOK TIME: 30 min.

CARBS: 36 g | FAT: 6 g | PROTEIN: 7 g | CALORIES: 223

INGREDIENTS

- *5 lb russet potatoes, peeled and cubed*
- *2 Tbsp butter*
- *1 tsp garlic powder*
- *1 cup whipping cream*
- *8-ounce cream cheese*
- *½ cup Cheddar cheese shredded*
- *Salt and black pepper, to taste*

DIRECTIONS

1. Let the potatoes boil in a big pot of salted water. Simmer for 20 minutes until tender. Drain the potatoes completely. Transfer to a large bowl.
2. Preheat the oven to 350°F.
3. Mash the potatoes with a potato masher until very fine. Add cream cheese and mash until fully incorporated. Add enough whipping cream to get a spoonable but smooth mixture.
4. Stir in the garlic powder and cheese. Add salt and pepper to taste.
5. Spray a 9x13-inch baking dish.
6. Spoon the mashed potatoes into the baking dish.
7. Dot the potatoes with butter and bake in the preheated oven for 30 minutes until the top is golden.
8. Let it sit for 5-10 minutes. Serve immediately!

PIZZA CASSEROLE

SERVINGS: 8 | PREP TIME: 20 min. | COOK TIME: 25 min.

CARBS: 66 g | FAT: 20 g | PROTEIN: 22 g | CALORIES: 511

INGREDIENTS

- *8 cheese biscuits (Cheese Biscuits recipe)*
- *8 oz. pizza sauce (Easy Pizza Sauce recipe)*
- *3 cups Mozzarella cheese shredded, divided*
- *1 tsp pizza seasoning*
- *Preferred pizza toppings*

DIRECTIONS

1. Preheat the oven to 375°F.
2. Cut 8 biscuits into 8 parts each and add to a bowl and mix with all of the pizza sauce and 1½ cups Mozzarella. Mix well and pour the prepared mixture into a greased 9x13-inch baking dish. Top with 1½ cups cheese and pepperoni slices.
3. Bake for 18-22 minutes or until golden brown and the cheese begins to brown.
4. Serve immediately!

CHEESE POTATO CASSEROLE

SERVINGS: 10 | PREP TIME: 20 min. | COOK TIME: 20 min.

CARBS: 29 g | FAT: 8 g | PROTEIN: 11 g | CALORIES: 236

INGREDIENTS

- *Canola oil cooking spray*
- *2 lbs red potatoes, peeled and diced*
- *1 cup low-fat milk*
- *2 Tbsp cornstarch*
- *2 cups Cheddar cheese, shredded*
- *1 cup non-fat Greek yogurt*
- *1 medium onion, chopped*
- *½ tsp + 1 pinch of salt, divided*
- *½ tsp black pepper*

DIRECTIONS

1. Preheat the oven to 350°F. Spray a 9x13-inch baking dish.
2. Add the potatoes to a large pot of water and bring to a boil. Immediately drain and rinse with cold water; drain well. Put back in the pot.
3. Whisk the cornstarch and milk and in a saucepan and bring to a boil over a medium-high heat, whisking for 3-4 minutes until thickened enough to coat the back of a spoon. Turn off the heat and stir in the yogurt, Cheddar, onion, ½ tsp salt, and pepper until combined. Pour the prepared mixture over the potatoes and mix well to coat. Spread evenly in the prepared baking dish.
4. Bake for 1 hour until golden-brown on top and the edges have browned. Take out of the oven and let it cool for 20 minutes before serving.

MINI HAM AND CHEESE MUFFINS

SERVINGS: 45 | PREP TIME: 30 min. | COOK TIME: 30 min.

CARBS: 2 g | FAT: 12 g | PROTEIN: 14 g | CALORIES: 184

INGREDIENTS

- *1¾ cup self-raising flour*
- *1 tsp baking powder*
- *3 slices ham, chopped*
- *6 fresh sage leaves, finely chopped*
- *⅓ cup Cheddar, chopped*
- *¼ cup unsalted butter, melted and cooled*
- *1 medium egg, beaten*
- *1½ Tbsp wholegrain mustard*
- *⅔ cup semi-skimmed milk*

DIRECTIONS

1. Preheat the oven to 400°F.
2. Sift the flour, baking powder, and ¼ tsp salt in a large bowl. Add the sage, ham, and cheddar. Form a well in the middle, then add the egg, mustard, butter, and milk. Mix until just combined.
3. Divide the mixture evenly among petits fours cases with a teaspoon, so that each is ¾ full. Transfer the cases onto two large baking sheets.
4. Bake for 8-10 minutes. Take out onto the wire racks and let it cool for 5 minutes.
5. Serve warm with your favorite dipping sauce.

ENGLISH MUFFINS

SERVINGS: 18 | PREP TIME: 25 min. | COOK TIME: 1 h. 50 min.

CARBS: 34 g | FAT: 3 g | PROTEIN: 5 g | CALORIES: 190

INGREDIENTS

- *1 cup milk*
- *2 Tbsp white sugar*
- *1 (.25 ounce) package active dry yeast*
- *1 cup warm water (110°F)*
- *¼ cup melted shortening*
- *6 cups all-purpose flour*
- *1 tsp salt*

DIRECTIONS

1. Warm the milk in a saucepan until it starts to bubble, remove from the heat. Add the sugar, stirring until dissolved. Let it cool until lukewarm.
2. In a bowl, mix the yeast in warm water until dissolved. Let it stand for 10 minutes.
3. Mix the milk, shortening, yeast mixture, and 3 cups flour in a large bowl. Beat until smooth. Add the salt and more flour until you make a soft dough while kneading. Transfer to a greased bowl, cover, and let it rise. Dust waxed paper with cornmeal.
4. Punch down. Roll the dough out to ½-inch thick. Cut rounds using a biscuit cutter and place the rounds on dusted waxed paper. Dust the tops with cornmeal. Cover, using plastic wrap, and let rise for 30 minutes.
5. Preheat a greased griddle. Cook the muffins for 10 minutes on each side at a medium heat until they have all been cooked.
6. Let them cool completely before serving or wrapping in a plastic bag.

CHEESE BISCUITS

SERVINGS: 15 | PREP TIME: 10 min. | COOK TIME: 20 min.

CARBS: 16 g | FAT: 10 g | PROTEIN: 4 g | CALORIES: 170

INGREDIENTS

- *2 cups Unbleached Self-Rising Flour*
- *4 ounces cheddar cheese*
- *1 cup heavy cream*

DIRECTIONS

1. Set a rack in the upper third, preheat the oven to 425°F.
2. Cut the cheese into chunks. Add the cheese and flour into the bowl of a food processor. Process until you get a smooth mixture.
3. Add the cream, and pulse until your dough starts to become cohesive. Transfer to a lightly floured work surface.
4. Pat the dough into a disc ¾-inch to 1-inch thick. The thicker you make them, the taller they will be.
5. Use a cutter to cut rounds. Place them on a parchment-lined baking sheet. Brush the tops with cream.
6. Bake for 15-18 minutes, until golden brown.
7. Remove from the oven and serve immediately.

CRUNCHY COOKIES

SERVINGS: 60 | PREP TIME: 10 min. | COOK TIME: 30 min.

CARBS: 12 g | FAT: 6 g | PROTEIN: 1 g | CALORIES: 120

INGREDIENTS

- *2 cups all-purpose flour*
- *⅔ cup unsalted butter, cold, cut into cubes*
- *1 large egg, lightly whisked*
- *1 tsp salt*
- *1 tsp granulated sugar*
- *1 tsp nigella seeds*
- *1 tsp sesame seeds*
- *1 egg yolk*
- *1 tsp water*

DIRECTIONS

1. Mix the salt, flour, and sugar in a bowl.
2. Add the butter to the flour mixture. Rub gently with your fingertips until it looks like breadcrumbs.
3. Add the egg and bring the dough together carefully with a spatula.
4. Divide in half and form balls. Cover each ball using plastic film, flatten them, and put them in the fridge for 20 minutes.
5. Preheat the oven to 350°F. Line with a parchment paper baking sheet. Remove the dough balls from the fridge.
6. Flour the work surface, rolling pin, and dough. Roll out the dough almost 8,5x7-inch long, ¼-inch thick. Use a 1½-inch cookie cutter. Roll out the dough from the leftovers. Repeat for the second half of the dough.
7. Mix the egg yolk and 1 tsp water to make an egg wash. Brush the cookies with the egg wash. Sprinkle all of the seeds on top.
8. Bake for 11-12 minutes until shiny and firm. Let them cool for 5 minutes on the baking sheet, then put them on a wire rack to completely cool.

ITALIAN STYLE BISCUITS

SERVINGS: 6 | PREP TIME: 10 min. | COOK TIME: 15 min.

CARBS: 12 g | FAT: 9 g | PROTEIN: 2 g | CALORIES: 121

INGREDIENTS

For the seasoning:
- *1 tsp garlic powder*
- *1 tsp onion powder*
- *1 tsp smoked paprika*
- *½ tsp oregano leaves, dried*
- *¼ tsp parsley leaves, dried*
- *¼ tsp marjoram leaves, dried*
- *¼ tsp basil leaves, dried*
- *1 tsp rock salt*
- *2 Tbsp Parmesan cheese, grated*

For the biscuits:
- *⅔ cup water*
- *2 cups plain flour*
- *⅓ cup olive oil + extra for brushing*
- *1 tsp baking powder*

DIRECTIONS

1. Preheat the oven to 200°F.
2. Add all of the seasoning components to a mortar and grind well.
3. Add the baking powder, flour, water, and oil to the bowl and mix until well combined.
4. Transfer to a floured work surface. Knead the dough briefly and divide into 3 portions. Roll each dough piece out on a floured surface, as thin as possible. Be careful not to tear. Cut shapes with a biscuit cutter.
5. Arrange the shapes on a lined oven tray, brush with olive oil and sprinkle with seasoning and cheese.
6. Bake for 10-12 minutes until browned. Serve immediately.

MUSHROOM AND CHICKEN PUFF PIE

SERVINGS: 6 | PREP TIME: 45 min. | COOK TIME: 30 min.

CARBS: 57 g | FAT: 47 g | PROTEIN: 55 g | CALORIES: 855

INGREDIENTS

- *1 Tbsp vegetable oil*
- *8 skinless boneless chicken thighs*
- *8 smoked bacon, cut into large pieces*
- *1 onion, halved and sliced*
- *1 cup baby button mushrooms*
- *1 handful of thyme sprigs*
- *2 Tbsp plain flour*
- *1 ⅔ cups chicken stock*
- *1 cup milk*
- *1 lb fresh puff pastry*
- *1 egg, beaten*

DIRECTIONS

1. Heat the oil in a frying pan over a medium-high heat. Season the thighs and fry for 5-8 minutes flipping infrequently until golden brown. Do it in batches if needed.
2. Transfer the chicken onto a plate and add the bacon into the pan. Fry for 5 minutes until crisp. Add the mushrooms, onion, and thyme sprigs, fry on a high heat for 3 more minutes. Tip the flour into the pan and cook for 1 minute, stirring. Remove from the heat.
3. Next, slowly stir in the chicken stock, milk, and put the chicken back into the pan.
4. Let it boil and simmer for 30 minutes. Spoon the filling into a large baking dish with a lip and let it cool.
5. Preheat the oven to 430°F. On a floured surface, roll the pastry to 1 coin thickness. Cut a long strip as wide as the rim of your baking dish and fix it to the dish edge with a little beaten egg. Brush with beaten egg, and top the pie with the pastry over it. Press the edges with your fingers and trim with a knife.
6. Brush the whole top with egg and bake for 30 minutes until it is risen and dark golden brown.

CHICKEN AND SWEETCORN PIE

SERVINGS: 6 | PREP TIME: 10 min. | COOK TIME: 35 min.

CARBS: 33 g | FAT: 32 g | PROTEIN: 19 g | CALORIES: 488

INGREDIENTS

- *1 lb puff pastry*
- *Flour for dusting*
- *2 skinless cooked chicken breasts*
- *3 Tbsp sweetcorn*
- *3 Tbsp frozen peas, defrosted*
- *6 Tbsp double cream*
- *1 tsp Dijon mustard*
- *1 egg, beaten*
- *Oil for brushing*

DIRECTIONS

1. Preheat the oven to 360°F.
2. Roll out the pastry on a dusted surface and trim to make a rectangle about 10x14-inch.
3. Cut the pastry in half lengthways and cut each half evenly into 3 squares, about 5-inch along each side, using scissors.
4. Push each square into the oiled tin, checking if it's pushed right into the edges.
5. With scissors, cut the chicken into strips, and then into chunks. Put them in a bowl. Add the peas, sweetcorn, mustard, and cream. Mix well.
6. Divide the mixture between the pies. Cover the tops of the pies with more rolled-out dough and press the edges to seal.
7. Brush the pastry with beaten egg. Bake for 35 minutes or until brown and the filling is bubbling.

HAM AND CHEESE QUICHE

SERVINGS: 8 | PREP TIME: 15 min. | COOK TIME: 45 min.

CARBS: 12 g | FAT: 31 g | PROTEIN: 20 g | CALORIES: 423

INGREDIENTS

- *1 pie crust*
- *1 cup light cream*
- *6 large eggs beaten*
- *¼ tsp salt*
- *¼ tsp pepper*
- *¼ tsp smoked paprika*
- *2 cloves garlic, minced*
- *1 cup cubed ham*
- *1 cup shredded Cheddar cheese*
- *1 cup grated Parmesan cheese*
- *1 cup spinach, chopped*
- *¼ cup green onion, chopped*
- *8 slices bacon, cooked and chopped*

DIRECTIONS

1. Preheat the oven to 350°F.
2. Place the crust on a plate pie (9-inch) and set aside.
3. Whisk the eggs, cream, garlic, paprika, salt, and pepper in a bowl. Set aside.
4. Arrange half of the cheddar cheese in one layer onto the bottom of the pie. Add the ham, parmesan cheese, green onion, bacon, and the second half of the cheddar cheese. Pour the egg mixture over the top.
5. Bake for 41-51 minutes until a toothpick inserted into the middle of the quiche comes out clean.
6. Let the quiche stand for 10 minutes before cutting and serving.

AUSSIE MEAT PIE

SERVINGS: 6 | PREP TIME: 15 min. | COOK TIME: 40 min.

CARBS: 36 g | FAT: 37 g | PROTEIN: 10 g | CALORIES: 715

INGREDIENTS

- 1 onion finely chopped
- 2 cups beef mince
- 1 cup water
- 2 beef stock cubes
- ¼ cup tomato sauce
- 2 tsp Worcestershire sauce
- 1 pinch salt and pepper *to taste
- 3 Tbsp plain flour
- 1 sheet shortcrust pastry
- 1 sheet puff pastry
- 1 egg to glaze

DIRECTIONS

1. Cook the meat and onion in a preheated oiled skillet over a medium-high heat until the meat is well browned, for 5-8 minutes or so.
2. Add ¾ cup water, sauces, stock cubes, and seasonings.
3. Let it boil and simmer for 15 minutes.
4. Blend the flour and ¼ cup water, stir into the meat and bring to a boil again. Simmer for 5 minutes. Remove from the heat and let it cool.
5. Line a pie plate with pastry. Spoon in the chilled meat filling. Moisten the pastry edges with water.
6. Top with puff pastry, sealing the edges, then trim and glaze with beaten egg.
7. Bake at 450°F for 15 minutes. Lower the heat to 380°F and bake for 25 more minutes until golden on top.
8. Take out of the oven and serve immediately.

PIZZA

NO-KNEAD PIZZA DOUGH

SERVINGS: 2 | PREP TIME: 2 h. 5 min. | COOK TIME: 15 min.

CARBS: 23 g | FAT: 5 g | PROTEIN: 4 g | CALORIES: 159

INGREDIENTS

- *4 cups flour*
- *1½ tsp instant yeast*
- *1½ tsp salt*
- *1½ cups lukewarm water*
- *1 tsp olive oil*

DIRECTIONS

1. Mix the flour, yeast, and salt in a bowl with a wooden spoon until well combined. Add all of the water and mix for 1 minute until it comes together and cleans the sides of the bowl. There is no need to knead it, all of the ingredients should be just mixed. The dough should come out soft and slightly sticky, with no streaks of flour on the surface.
2. Grease a large mixing bowl with oil. With floured hands, form a ball from the dough. Place it into the prepared bowl and turn around a few times to coat it with oil.
3. Cover using plastic wrap and leave for 3 hours at room temperature to double in size.
4. Once risen, you can shape the dough into pizzas and bake it.

PEPPERONI PIZZA

SERVINGS: 1 | PREP TIME: 15 min. | COOK TIME: 15 min.

CARBS: 35 g | FAT: 13 g | PROTEIN: 12 g | CALORIES: 313

INGREDIENTS

- *1 pizza dough (No-Knead Pizza Dough recipe)*
- *½ cup pizza sauce (Easy Pizza Sauce recipe)*
- *20 slices pepperoni*
- *¼ cup chopped pepperoni*
- *12 ounces mozzarella cheese, grated*
- *½ tsp ground black pepper*
- *1 tsp fresh oregano, optional*
- *Flour for rolling and shaping dough*
- *¼ cup softened butter*
- *2 Tbsp honey*

DIRECTIONS

1. Preheat the oven to 500°F.
2. Roll out the dough on a dusted surface, then press it into a large cast-iron pan.
3. Spread the sauce over the dough, leaving ¼-inch crust around the edges. Sprinkle chopped pepperoni over the sauce. Next, sprinkle with grated cheese and top with sliced pepperoni. Season with black pepper.
4. Bake for 12-15 minutes until the crust is golden brown.
5. Serve immediately!

HAWAIIAN PIZZA

SERVINGS: 1 | PREP TIME: 15 min. | COOK TIME: 15 min.

CARBS: 38 g | FAT: 8 g | PROTEIN: 14 g | CALORIES: 270

INGREDIENTS

- Semolina flour for dusting
- 1 pizza dough (_No-Knead Piazza Dough_ recipe)
- 8 Tbsp pizza sauce (_Easy Pizza Sauce_ recipe)
- 6 slices cooked ham, ripped into pieces
- 0.5 oz can or freshly sliced and diced pineapple
- 1 ball mozzarella, ripped into pieces
- Olive oil

DIRECTIONS

1. Put a baking tray on the bottom shelf and preheat the oven to 500°F.
2. Sprinkle some semolina on a working surface and roll out the dough with a rolling pin, 12 inches in diameter. Do not roll it too thick.
3. Press the dough into your cast-iron skillet and spread the sauce onto the pizza. Leave a ¼-inch border sauce-free. Top with ham, pineapple, and mozzarella.
4. Bake for 13-14 minutes until the cheese has melted and it has a golden crispy crust. Drizzle with 1 Tbsp olive oil and serve.

ENGLISH MUFFIN PIZZAS

CARBS: 14 g | FAT: 5 g | PROTEIN: 7 g | CALORIES: 123

INGREDIENTS

- *6 English muffins (<u>English Muffins</u> recipe), halved*
- *15 ounces Pizza sauce (<u>Easy Pizza Sauce</u> recipe)*
- *8 ounces shredded Mozzarella Cheese*
- *½ cup sliced pepperoni*
- *¼ cup chopped parsley*

DIRECTIONS

1. Preheat the oven to 400°F.
2. Arrange the muffin halves on a baking sheet facing up.
3. Spread pizza sauce on top of each half, sprinkle with cheese, and then layer the pepperoni.
4. Bake for 15 minutes or so until the cheese has melted.
5. Sprinkle with chopped parsley and serve!

EASY PIZZA SAUCE

SERVINGS: 1 | PREP TIME: 5 min. | COOK TIME: 5 min.

CARBS: 70 g | FAT: 30 g | PROTEIN: 16 g | CALORIES: 549

INGREDIENTS

- *1 garlic clove, minced*
- *1 14 ounce can crushed tomatoes in puree*
- *1 Tbsp olive oil*
- *½ tsp brown sugar*
- *½ tsp Italian seasoning*
- *½ tsp dried basil*
- *1 pinch of salt*
- *1 pinch of crushed red pepper flakes*

DIRECTIONS

1. Sauté the garlic in oil in a small saucepan until tender.
2. Stir in the rest of the ingredients and let it boil then turn the heat to low.
3. Simmer for 12-15 minutes, uncovered, until it's the desired thickness.
4. You can keep the sauce in the fridge for up to 1 week.

PIZZA ROLLS

SERVINGS: 12 | PREP TIME: 10 min. | COOK TIME: 15 min.

CARBS: 19 g | FAT: 6 g | PROTEIN: 7 g | CALORIES: 150

INGREDIENTS

- *1 pizza dough (No-Knead Piazza Dough recipe)*
- *½ tsp garlic salt*
- *1 tsp dried basil*
- *1 cup shredded mozzarella cheese*
- *¼ cup shredded Parmesan cheese*
- *½ cup sliced pepperoni, chopped*
- *1 cup pizza sauce (Easy Pizza Sauce recipe)*
- *½ cup chopped parsley*

DIRECTIONS

1. Preheat the oven to 425°F.
2. Press your pizza dough into a large rectangle.
3. Sprinkle with garlic salt, basil, cheese, and pepperoni. Tightly roll the dough up to form a log, starting at the long end. Slice the log into 1-inch pieces. Arrange the rolls on greased baking sheets.
4. Bake for 10-12 minutes until the top has browned.
5. Serve with warm pizza sauce for dipping and sprinkle with parsley.

PARMESAN PIZZA STICKS

SERVINGS: 6 | PREP TIME: 10 min. | COOK TIME: 20 min.

CARBS: 38 g | FAT: 18 g | PROTEIN: 22 g | CALORIES: 400

INGREDIENTS

- *1 pizza dough (No-Knead Piazza Dough recipe)*
- *6 mozzarella string cheese sticks*
- *⅔ cup mini pepperoni*
- *1 cup Parmesan cheese, grated*
- *1 cup pizza sauce (Easy Pizza Sauce recipe)*

DIRECTIONS

1. Preheat the oven to 400°F. Line a baking sheet with parchment paper.
2. Roll the pizza dough (1-inch thick) and slice into 6 pieces. Slice string cheese down the middle of each piece and stuff with pepperoni.
3. Wrap each stuffed string cheese in dough. Place on the prepared baking sheet and sprinkle with Parmesan.
4. Bake for 15-20 minutes until golden brown. Let it cool for 3-5 minutes.
5. Warm pizza sauce in a saucepan and serve with the pizza sticks.

FLAKY PUFF PASTRY

SERVINGS: 2 sheets | PREP TIME: 45 min. | COOK TIME: none

CARBS: 25 g | FAT: 18 g | PROTEIN: 3 g | CALORIES: 271

INGREDIENTS

- *¾ cup butter at room temperature, divided into 4 portions and cubed*
- *1 ¾ cups all-purpose flour, sieved*
- *1 pinch of salt*
- *¼-½ cup cold water*
- *2 Tbsp sugar*

DIRECTIONS

1. Mix the flour, sugar, and salt in a bowl. Don't add the sugar if you want to cook a savory dish.
2. Add 1 portion of butter to the flour mixture and, while slowly adding enough cold water, incorporate the butter and flour with a round-bladed knife until an elastic dough starts to form.
3. Dust your working surface, and turn the dough out. Roll it out into a rectangle and roll until you get a 4-mm thickness. Add more flour to avoid sticking (if needed).
4. Remove the excess flour from your surface and add the next portion of butter, by dotting it evenly on ⅔ of the rolled out pastry.
5. Fold the pastry, bringing the end without butter to the center, then cover it with the other third.
6. Press the pastry edges together with your fingers, turn the pastry half a turn and roll it out lightly until it's 4 mm thick.
7. Repeat steps 4-6 two times, fold into three as the 5 step says, and put in the fridge for 30 minutes, tightly covered with a plastic wrap.
8. Next, use the dough for your recipe or freeze until ready to use.
9. If you use frozen dough, let it defrost in the fridge before cooking.

TARTS FINES WITH CARAMEL CRISP

SERVINGS: 6 | PREP TIME: 30 min. | COOK TIME: 30 min.

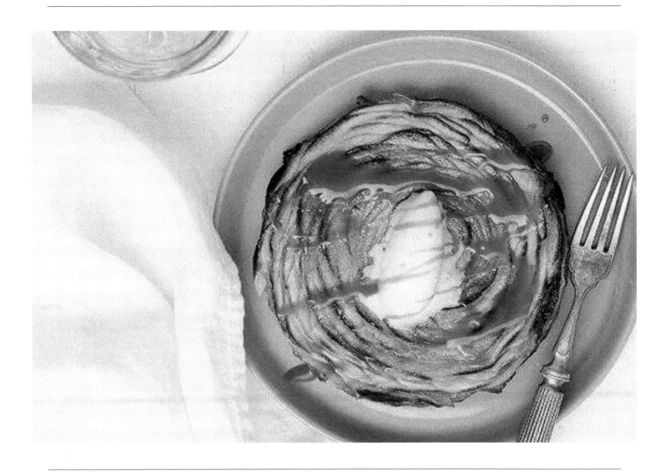

CARBS: 38 g | FAT: 5 g | PROTEIN: 3 g | CALORIES: 210

INGREDIENTS

- *1 lb puff pastry (Flaky Puff Pastry recipe)*
- *plain flour for dusting*
- *4 crisp apples, quartered, cored and sliced very finely*
- *½ cup caster sugar, plus extra for sprinkling*
- *¼ cup melted butter*
- *1 egg, beaten, to glaze*
- *½ cup apricot jam, to glaze*
- *Vanilla ice cream, to serve*

For the caramel:
- *½ cup water*
- *½ cup sugar*

DIRECTIONS

1. Preheat the oven to 400°F.
2. Roll the pastry out on a dusted surface to a 4-mm thickness, and cut out circles (6 x 12cm). Transfer to a baking sheet, prick each circle over with a fork, and put in the fridge for 10 minutes to chill.
3. Sprinkle the circles with caster sugar, top each one with overlapping layers of sliced apples, leaving a 1-inch free space around the edge.
4. Brush the apples with melted butter and dust with sugar. Brush the border of the pastry with egg.
5. Bake for 15 minutes until golden. Remove from the oven and brush the tops with apricot glaze. Set aside.
6. To make the caramel, carefully heat 100g sugar with 100ml water in a pan until the sugar has melted. Increase the heat and let it bubble for 5 minutes until it's a dark golden caramel color.
7. Put enough ice cream on top of each tart and drizzle the caramel over them with a spoon. Let it set and crisp up for 2-3 minutes. Serve immediately.

FRUIT PUFF PASTRY

SERVINGS: 7 | PREP TIME: 30 min. | COOK TIME: 15 min.

CARBS: 32 g | FAT: 16 g | PROTEIN: 3 g | CALORIES: 267

INGREDIENTS

- *1 lb puff pastry (Flaky Puff Pastry recipe)*
- *1 jar jam*
- *1 egg*
- *1 tsp heavy cream*
- *1 Tbsp coarse sugar*
- *1 cup confectioners' sugar*
- *2 Tbsp heavy cream*
- *1 tsp vanilla extract*

DIRECTIONS

1. Roll the pastry out onto a lightly dusted surface.
2. Cut out hearts with a heart-shaped cookie cutter.
3. Whisk the egg and heavy cream in a small bowl to make an egg wash. Brush the outer edges of half of the hearts with egg wash.
4. Spoon 1½ Tbsp jam onto the center of egg-washed hearts. Cover the filling with the second half of the hearts. Press the edges of the hearts with a fork to seal them.
5. Arrange the hearts on a baking sheet lined with parchment paper, and put into the freezer for 20 minutes.
6. Meanwhile, preheat the oven to 400°F.
7. Once the pastry has chilled, brush with the rest of the egg wash and sprinkle with coarse sugar.
8. Bake for 15-20 minutes until puffy and golden-brown.
9. Let them cool for 5 minutes before serving.

APPLE CINNAMON PASTRY

SERVINGS: 6 | PREP TIME: 1 h. | COOK TIME: 30 min.

CARBS: 7 g | FAT: 6 g | PROTEIN: 2 g | CALORIES: 91

INGREDIENTS

- *2 Tbsp sugar*
- *¼ tsp cinnamon*
- *1 cup diced apples, skin on*
- *3 Tbsp raisins*
- *1 egg beaten*
- *1 lb puff pastry sheets (<u>Flaky Puff Pastry</u> recipe)*
- *1 Tbsp powdered sugar*

DIRECTIONS

1. Mix the sugar and cinnamon in a bowl and set aside. Add the apples and raisins, toss well to coat everything evenly.
2. Roll the puff pastry out onto a floured working surface. Cut into 4x3-inch rectangles. Brush around the perimeter of each rectangle with beaten egg.
3. Fill each piece with 1½ Tbsp apple mixture on half of the dough. Top with the second half of the dough and seal with your fingers, pressing down into the pastry all the way around.
4. Brush the tops with egg, and cut 3 slits across the apple mound. Place pastry on a parchment-lined sheet. Put in the fridge for 20 minutes.
5. Preheat the oven to 400°F. Bake for 25-30 minutes.
6. Take out of the oven and let it cool slightly then serve.

NUTELLA PUFF PASTRY

SERVINGS: 9 | PREP TIME: 10 min. | COOK TIME: 15 min.

CARBS: 15 g | FAT: 11 g | PROTEIN: 3 g | CALORIES: 167

INGREDIENTS

- *1-2 sheets puff pastry (Flaky Puff Pastry recipe)*
- *1 egg whisked*
- *2 Tbsp sugar granulated*
- *Nutella Spread as much as needed*

DIRECTIONS

1. Preheat the oven to 400°F. Using parchment paper, line a baking sheet.
2. Put two pastry sheets on top of each other and roll them with a pin to make one large dough. Brush the dough with egg. Sprinkle with half the sugar and cut into 9 squares.
3. Place 1 Tbsp Nutella in the center of each square. Firmly pinch the two opposite ends of each square and flatten the pinched ends. Brush with the rest of the egg and sprinkle the rest of the sugar on top.
4. Bake for 12-15 minutes, rotating the sheet after 6-8 minutes until deep golden in color.
5. Add 1 Tbsp Nutella to a Ziplock bag, heat it for 10 seconds, cut the corner of the bag, and drizzle on top of each pastry. Serve immediately.

NO-BAKE CINNAMON ROLLS

SERVINGS: 4 | PREP TIME: 15 min. | COOK TIME: 15 min.

CARBS: 16 g | FAT: 6 g | PROTEIN: 1 g | CALORIES: 124

INGREDIENTS

- *2 slices white bread, crusts removed*
- *2 Tbsp butter*
- *2 Tbsp cinnamon sugar*
- *2 Tbsp confectioners' sugar*
- *⅛ tsp water, or as needed*

DIRECTIONS

1. Roll the bread slices until they become very flat. Butter the flattened bread and sprinkle it with cinnamon sugar. Roll up the bread slice until tight, starting on one side. Repeat with the second bread slice. Cut the prepared bread rolls into 1-inch slices.
2. Mix water and confectioners' sugar in a small bowl. Drizzle the frosting over the slices and serve.

RASPBERRY CHEESECAKE BARS

SERVINGS: 12 | PREP TIME: 20 min. | COOK TIME: 1 h. 10 min.

CARBS: 19 g | FAT: 16 g | PROTEIN: 2 g | CALORIES: 227

INGREDIENTS

For the crust:
- *2 cups shortbread cookies*
- *½ cup melted salted butter*
- *2 Tbsp sugar*

For the filling:
- *16-ounce cream cheese, softened*
- *1 cup sugar*
- *1 ¼ cups fresh raspberries*
- *1 cup fresh heavy cream*
- *1 tsp vanilla*

For the garnish:
- *¼ cup fresh raspberries*
- *fresh whipped cream*

DIRECTIONS

1. Using parchment paper, line an 8x8-inch square baking pan.
2. Mix the cookie crumbs, melted butter, and sugar in a bowl until crumbs form.
3. Press the crumb mixture into the bottom of the lined pan. Put in the freezer for 30 minutes.
4. Add the raspberries and sugar to the food processor bowl. Leave for 15 minutes to let the berries get juicy. Then, pulse until smooth. Press the berry puree through a fine-mesh strainer, discarding the seeds and pulp. Stir in the sugar and set aside.
5. Add the cream cheese and sugar to a mixer. Mix until completely creamy.
6. Whip the heavy cream in a different bowl until soft peaks start to form. Fold it into the prepared cream cheese mixture.
7. Take the crust out of the freezer and pour the filling all over it. Dollop berry puree on top of cheesecake with a spoon. Make swirls with a skewer.
8. Cover and leave in the freezer overnight.
9. Cut into slices, top with raspberries, and serve cold.

MINI APPLE PIE BITES

SERVINGS: 30 | PREP TIME: 20 min. | COOK TIME: 15 min.

CARBS: 7 g | FAT: 2 g | PROTEIN: 1 g | CALORIES: 41

INGREDIENTS

- *1 Tbsp unsalted butter*
- *3 Honeycrisp apples, peeled, cored, and diced*
- *1 tsp cinnamon*
- *⅛ tsp each salt and nutmeg*
- *¼ cup dark brown sugar, packed*
- *⅓ cup water*
- *1 tsp lemon juice*
- *3 Tbsp cornstarch*
- *⅓ cup waterbites*
- *30 mini phyllo shells*
- *Whipped cream, as much as needed*
- *Salted caramel sauce, as much as needed*

DIRECTIONS

1. Preheat the oven to 350°F.
2. Melt the butter in a pan over a medium heat. Add the apples, cinnamon, salt, nutmeg, and sugar. Stir well and add water. Let it boil and turn the heat to low. Simmer covered, until the apples have softened slightly (5-6 minutes). Turn to a medium-low heat and cook for 5-6 minutes uncovered.
3. At the same time, whisk the water and cornstarch in a small bowl until dissolved. Pour the dissolved cornstarch into the apples and stir to combine. Cook for 2-3 minutes more until thickened. Mix in lemon juice and take off the heat. Let it cool for 5-10 minutes.
4. Arrange the phyllo shells on a baking sheet and bake for 3-5 minutes until crisp. Remove from the oven.
5. Spoon the apple filling into each shell. Top with whipped cream, drizzle with caramel and sprinkle with cinnamon before serving.

NO-BAKE CHOCOLATE CHIP COOKIE BARS

SERVINGS: 16 | PREP TIME: 10 min. | COOK TIME: 3 h.

CARBS: 11 g | FAT: 5 g | PROTEIN: 1 g | CALORIES: 80

INGREDIENTS

For the base layer:
- *½ cup unsalted butter, softened*
- *1 cup packed light brown sugar*
- *1 tsp vanilla extract*
- *⅓ cup milk*
- *½ tsp salt*
- *2 ⅓ cups oat flour*
- *1 cup mini chocolate chips*

For the ganache topping:
- *1½ cups chocolate chips*
- *2 Tbsp coconut oil*

DIRECTIONS

1. Cream the butter and brown sugar with an electric mixer in a bowl until well combined. Beat in the milk, vanilla extract, salt, and flour. Mix until smooth. Fold in the chocolate chips.
2. With wax paper, line an 8x8-inch baking pan. Spread the prepared dough out evenly, filling with all corners of the pan. Put in the fridge for 2-3 hours.
3. When the prepared dough is solid, melt the rest of the chocolate chips with coconut oil over low heat in a small saucepan until smooth. Let it chill for 2-3 minutes.
4. Pour over the dough and spread evenly. Put the pan back in the fridge for 20 minutes to solidify the chocolate.
5. Slice into squares and serve immediately.

CONCLUSION

Thank you for reading this book and having the patience to try the recipes.

I do hope that you have had as much enjoyment reading and experimenting with the meals as I have had writing the book.

Stay safe and healthy!

RECIPE INDEX

Dry Weights

oz	(spoon)	C	(scale) g	(scale) lb
1/2 OZ	1 Tbsp	1/16 C	15 g	
1 OZ	2 Tbsp	1/8 C	28 g	
2 OZ	4 Tbsp	1/4 C	57 g	
3 OZ	6 Tbsp	1/3 C	85 g	
4 OZ	8 Tbsp	1/2 C	115 g	1/4 lb
8 OZ	16 Tbsp	1 C	227 g	1/2 lb
12 OZ	24 Tbsp	1 1/2 C	340 g	3/4 lb
16 OZ	32 Tbsp	2 C	455 g	1 lb

Liquid Conversions

1 Gallon:
4 quarts
8 pints
16 cups
128 fl oz
3.8 liters

1 Quart:
2 pints
4 cups
32 fl oz
0.95 liters

1 Pint:
2 cups
16 fl oz
480 ml

1 Cup:
16 Tbsp
8 fl oz
240 ml

oz	(spoon)	(spoon)	mL	C	Pt	Qt
1 oz	6 tsp	2 Tbsp	30 ml	1/8 C		
2 oz	12 tsp	4 Tbsp	60 ml	1/4 C		
2 2/3 oz	16 tsp	5 Tbsp	80 ml	1/3 C		
4 oz	24 tsp	8 Tbsp	120 ml	1/2 C		
5 1/3 oz	32 tsp	11 Tbsp	160 ml	2/3 C		
6 oz	36 tsp	12 Tbsp	177 ml	3/4 C		
8 oz	48 tsp	16 Tbsp	237 ml	1 C	1/2 pt	1/4 qt
16 oz	96 tsp	32 Tbsp	480 ml	2 C	1 pt	1/2 qt
32 oz	192 tsp	64 Tbsp	950 ml	4 C	2 pt	1 qt

Fahrenheit to Celcius (F to C)

500 F = 260 C
475 F = 245 C
450 F = 235 C
425 F = 220 C
400 F = 205 C
375 F = 190 C
350 F = 180 C
325 F = 160 C
300 F = 150 C
275 F = 135 C
250 F = 120 C
225 F = 107 C

1 tsp: 5 ml

1 Tbsp: 15 ml

Safe Cooking Meat Temperatures

Minimum temperatures:

USDA Safe at 145 F	USDA Safe at 160 F	USDA Safe at 165 F
Beef Steaks, Briskets, and Roasts; Pork Chops, Roasts, Ribs, Shoulders, and Butts; Lamb Chops, Legs, and Roasts; Fresh Hams, Veal Steaks, Fish, and Shrimp	Ground Meats (except poultry)	Chicken & Turkey, ground or whole

CPSIA information can be obtained
at www.ICGtesting.com
Printed in the USA
BVHW060950151221
624023BV00009B/647